*To Cheryl
May God's blessing be yours always
Sincerely
Amy E. Tobin
Barb B...*

STILL, LOVE REMAINS
God's Crimson Threads of Grace

AMY E. TOBIN

Still, Love Remains
God's Crimson Threads of Grace
ISBN 978-0-9863907-0-8 Softcover
Printed in the United States of America

First Printing, 2015
21 20 19 18 17 16 15/7 6 5 4 3 2 1

God Is Good Foundation
425 W. Jennings St.
Newburgh, IN 47630
www.godisgoodfoundation.org

To
all who have walked this journey with me –
and to my God
who both preserves and beautifully redeems
my life.

I love you
&
Thank you

Acknowledgements

It is with immense gratitude that I say thank you to the following. Without their encouragement, blessings and assistance this book would not have been possible.

God – Thank you for redeeming my soul and restoring my heart. May my life, my breath and my talents bring you glory always.

My family – You keep me real

God Is Good Foundation – You believe in me

Nick Basham – For the cover and layout of the book

Joey Goebel – For editorial assistance

Crossroads Christian Church – You are a blessing to my heart

First Church of the Nazarene – Thank you for nourishing the seeds my dad planted. I am truly a life that was changed.

You, the reader – Thank you for choosing to read this story. May these pages be a blessing to you and may you be inspired to trace God's hand in the love story He writes in your journey of faith.

Contents

Preface

Beside a gently flowing river there is a charming little town. Within the town there is a person, and within the person, there is a story. It is not so much a tale of events which occurred one fateful morning almost four years ago when a father took the life of his child in a murder-suicide. No, instead, the story is that of the faithfulness of God who has woven His grace as a crimson thread of love against the darkness of the valley those events created.

As the mother of that child, that day redefined my life. Though it has been called by many a horrific tragedy, the tragedy would be simply not to allow God to be glorified in its wake. It left a cavern so deep, only through God would I be able to journey beyond its borders and into the light of a new day. Through the mercies of God I would experience life again, filled with beautiful horizons of joy.

Many say if we live long enough we will all somehow experience a valley in our life. At some point, everyone will need hope the difficulty will end and there will be something good, somehow, that comes because of it. This aspect is a story I can freely share.

I have changed the names contained within these pages to allow everyone touched by the events to continue upon their own healing journey toward peace. In this, we afford all the blessings of grace to find rest at the foot of the throne of God. We give each one the hope to move on to the fullness of each new day and extend an invitation for all to experience the beauty of the joys of tomorrows yet to be known.

We all have a story. We travel through life with its good and bad, joy and sorrow, challenges and peace. While this book shares a part of my journey, it also shares a God who is intimately involved in your own.

Valleys, difficulties, trials and hardships may come in life, but within them God creates a work of grace which He alone can do. God shapes, molds, heals, redeems, and restores. Within these pages a greater story is told regarding the matchless and unfailing love of God. He is and always will work in the midst of the *"every day"* to weave His crimson threads of redemption within every circumstance we meet.

Meeting Grace

She stood at the entrance of the doorway, her hand on the door. This beautiful precious child of mine.

"Come on Momma! The world awaits! We have new places to see and new things to do. Let's go find our adventure today and fill our hearts with memories."

The sun shined down on her shoulder length dark brown hair creating a touch of red highlights which complimented the bright yellow t-shirt and purple leggings she wore that day. Her white sneakers showed stains from the grass of adventures she had already known. Joy reflected in her deep brown eyes as she teased her new little kitten, Rosie, with the pink ribbon meant for her hair and she giggled.

Elisabeth Grace Tobin was an absolutely amazing child. A precocious little girl, she had a heart of gold and wisdom beyond her years. She loved to laugh, and she talked so much I teased her she wasn't built with an off button. *"Momma do you want me to zip it?"* she'd say sometimes, and we'd both laugh together.

In the seven years she spent on this earth she made a lifetime of memories. The lives of the people she met were changed forever because we knew her. Elisabeth was not a person who was to learn from us. No, we were to learn about God through knowing her. To a special few, she was to be a blessing that transformed our entire existence.

"Are you ready Momma?" she asked. *"Come on. Let's go see the world."* Elisabeth reached for my hand as I stood on the stairs smiling, looking at my sweet baby girl. A touch of pink nail polish still remained on her fingers from practicing her painting skills and her skin was beautifully tanned from plenty of summer fun.

She had captured my heart. My little miracle, the answer to five years of prayer to have a child, Elisabeth Grace was my world and the joy of my existence. Through her life I learned wonderful lessons of faith and knew beyond any doubt God heard and answered prayer. I understood nothing was impossible with God. Because of her I am a better person.

"*Ok sweetheart. Let's go make our own adventure,*" I responded.

We'd take a drive until we reached a place that looked like it would be a good area to stop. A park was our choice for this day. As we walked along the open space Elisabeth chattered away about all the possibilities that awaited us, on our journey through the field of the "*everlasting memory*" as she had dubbed today's trip together.

"*Where do you come up with these things child?*" I asked her as I laughed and she giggled, "*It's a gift Momma. God just made me that way.*" I laughed again.

"*Oh yes, God made you that way sweetheart just so I could do this....*" I grabbed her up and twirled her around until we both landed on the sloping hillside's soft blanket of grass. We laughed together as she kissed my cheek and said "*Momma, I love you.*" "*Love you too, baby girl.*" I responded as a grasshopper leaped from the ground near her hand and landed on her head.

It tickled her, and she laughed. "*Momma look! He likes me!*"

"*Well of course. Grasshoppers know a good thing when they see one!*" I said as she reached up to pluck him off and he hopped away. I reminded her I had a picture of something similar from several years back when another one had done the same thing. "*Bet you're one of only a handful of people in the world who get to have grasshoppers land on their head,*" I told her. Elisabeth laughed and turned her attention to chasing the monarch butterfly that flitted across our path on that warm summer day.

Wildflowers grew along our trail as the beauty of the park and her smile made a wonderful memory. Here in this one site existed ample opportunities to enjoy the marvelous creation all around us. The brilliant blue of the cloudless sky and the hot air balloon against the backdrop of the park would have been a picture in the making if I had brought along my camera.

"Ok baby girl, what do you say we grab some ice cream and head back home. We can play a game or two together or maybe, just maybe we might go for a swim. Would you like that?"

"Oh yes Momma, but what I'd really like to do... well, could we stop and pray?"

"Stop and pray?" I hadn't expected that, but it certainly was a proud momma moment. *"Well sure baby girl, what do you want to pray about?"*

"Aww Momma, let's thank God for giving us today. I bet that would make Him smile."

"I bet that would," I said. *"Would you like to talk to God for us this time, angel cake, since I said our breakfast prayer?"*

"Ok. But Momma," Elisabeth grinned, *"you know I'm Princess Strawberry Bliss."*

I laughed. *"Oh, ok Princess Strawberry Bliss."* In that moment, every beat of my heart deepened the love I had for Elisabeth Grace. With a curtsy in true Momma fashion I continued, *"God and all the court of heaven are waiting to hear from you, darling Princess Strawberry Bliss, the grand noble daughter of the Most High King."*

I once thought the world could only be changed by those who had lived long and great lives on the spotlight of the world's stage. This child showed me the grace of my God, the faithfulness of His presence throughout every circumstance, and that the God of all creation could write a story of His love upon the pages of my heart.

She giggled. *"God, you out did yourself today in making such a gorgeous day. Do you know how much I love you? I've enjoyed this. God, did you tell that grasshopper to jump on my head? And bring that butterfly so I could chase it? Thank you if you did. And thank you God for my Momma. Would you promise to take care of her and love on her too? Please. In Jesus name I ask. Oh and by the way please tell him I said hi. Amen."*

PART ONE

May God create strong foundations
of faith and may He forever hold
the throne of our heart.

Chapter 1

Beautiful Foundations

Today, I can tell you God is good, not because it is a phrase, but because I have experienced it. The person I was just four years ago no longer exists; a new me is growing, a deeper me. A person who was completely shattered and needed to relearn everything I once thought I knew. I had to glimpse myself in a mirror before a Holy God and my heart had to trust our Lord enough to cry out to Him, *"You see this book (the Bible); either you are who you say you are, or this book means nothing, because I NEED you."*

God prepares us all in some measure, for the difficult times our life may hold. In simple, yet precious experiences He would groom my heart. I needed foundations that could carry me through the valley God knew my life would one day hold. This gift of training would not come in the form of life experiences gained as an adult, but instead through the legacies of faith that would be instilled into my heart as a young girl sitting at the side of my father.

My mother and each member of my family played their own significant role in shaping who I would become. However, the one who had the most influence was my dad. Dad's heart and his walk with God weaved peacefully into connections with his family and friends. He enjoyed sharing things which would have a positive and distinctive influence.

Into moments together with my father, God would lace the threads of unassuming details into a background, and a way of thinking which would influence my perception. As God entwined each aspect of devotion into a fabric of a relationship, He would prepare me for a journey which would one day bring me to my knees. Yet, the same path would also come to reveal God's love on a deeper level than

1

I ever imagined, transforming completely the person I am.

I am from an eastern state, an exquisitely beautiful place of majestic mountains. The landscape becomes filled with breathtaking foliage, as the summer gives way to the glory of autumn, and scenic picturesque valleys dip gracefully into its terrain. Silently, the geography itself seems magnificently to allude to the valleys and mountain experiences in life.

In that region days are lived out in simplicity, as well as rugged adventure – almost heaven in its beauty, almost perfection in its charm. There is a strength that is woven into the people of this area. It is forged through the deep bonds of family and friendships. Then, this unites with faith. Through the subtle but meaningful influence of members of the quaint little churches that often dot the landscape, strength softly comes.

We lived in a modest little suburb of a good sized city. The local college football game was often the talk of our sleepy town. Here, the tiny grocery store around the corner had wooden floors, and the owners greeted us all by name.

Fifteen minutes away, we could step into the rolling hills of the countryside's open green pastures. Journey slightly beyond that, and the mountains rise up from the ground in all their pristine beauty. There, one lane roads are common and even outhouses can still be found.

We could even journey on a little farther still, over the mountain tops, deep into the rugged outdoors. In just an hour's drive we can reach areas where the driveways may be creek beds with flowing water. In those areas, the wilderness animals of bear, mountain lion and even the occasional panther can be found.

Into this humble setting, God began to write the story of life which would draw me to know Him and would keep me walking by His side. Through a background both peacefully sheltered and blessed, life was gloriously quiet.

A twenty-seven year age difference existed between my parents. A remarkable sweetness occurred in our family since I and my younger sister had been born so late in Dad's life. At sixty-one and sixty-two, becoming a father again brought him much joy.

My Mom, Sarah, was a nurse at one of the two local hospitals. She worked a swing shift, though – predominantly evenings. Dad retired from the local milk creamery when we began school. As the most available, Dad basically raised us, and he did so with the same old–fashioned values which marked his own childhood. We were free to do what we wanted as long as we stayed out of trouble and were within the range of the sound of Dad's whistle when he opened the door to call us home again.

About 5'7" and stout, Dad didn't stand out in a crowd. His thick gray hair was the envy of most men his age. Behind his glasses, Dad's dark brown eyes held a sparkle which reflected deep love for his family. The comforting scent of Old Spice his gentle soft spoken tone, calm but happy demeanor and genuine concern for others made Ralph Waldo Tobin the epitome of a dearly loved teddy bear. A man of deep faith, this remains his most defining quality.

I was a *"Daddy's girl."* I enjoyed being with him. We sat for many hours under the shelter of a covered patio delighting in the beauty all around us. The gentle breeze of the ceiling fan provided some relief from the humidity of the hot summer days.

In a swing so big I could lay in it to nap, I would listen to Dad tell stories of the *"good ole days."* He would rub my feet or place his arm around me tenderly as I snuggled up close beside him. World War II had taken a heavy toll on his hearing. Sometimes it was just better to listen. I'd enjoy the smile that graced his face as he spoke of faith and the stories of family members long since passed.

3

I'd ask him a question or two when something piqued my interest. This assured Dad that indeed, I had been taking note. Even though really, at times the soft and slow swaying motion of the swing gently lulled me to sleep.

As the beautiful winters would come each year, the fresh snowfall would stunningly adorn the mountains, hills and valleys with a delicate, almost ethereal elegance. Mostly, however, the valley protected our community from the deep snow falls of the mountains which could be measured in feet, not inches.

A rich family heritage of faith in Christ and generations of prayer became the legacies given to us. My family both acknowledged and taught that God is important. They donated their land for churches to be built and established. They led congregations, and they passed on the blessings of trusting God.

My dad read us Bible stories. A large picture hung on our wall of Jesus surrounded by children. Even in such a simple illustration my parents planted seeds that helped remind us we may always talk to our Lord.

Each Saturday evening, Dad would steal away to a place by himself to prepare for worship the next morning. He would read his Bible and study the lesson in the church devotional. This and his prayer time were the only moments Dad ushered us away from him for his time alone with God.

Dad taught us a growing relationship with Christ is important by living it out every single day. He brought it up in conversation so often that he was always instructing us – instilling within us the things he wanted us to know. From my earliest memories Dad built strong standing stones of faith, the markers which pointed the way to Christ and would carry me back again to Him when necessary.

As a girl, I saw my father pray every night on his knees. Out loud, he lifted the name of every member of his family to the throne of the Living God. I never liked to be away from my dad for too long, even during his prayer time and devotions.

If I interrupted, which to my father's frustration I often had a habit of doing, he allowed me to stand there. He didn't answer me until he had finished his conversation with God. Sometimes Dad locked himself in a room so he wouldn't be disturbed. This didn't always stop me from knocking on the door to spend time with him, however.

"Daddy, why don't you answer me when you pray?" I asked him one evening.

"Honey, it's important to always remember who you're speaking with when you pray. Others will be there when you're done. In this, you will make God the most important one of all in your heart."

"Why out loud Dad?"

"You can pray in your heart honey. This is how your Mommy prays and sometimes I do too, but I want to talk to God like I talk to you. He's always there Amy. We have a relationship. It hasn't always been so for me. There was a time when I didn't serve God. I talk to God because He's made a difference in me. Walk with Him Amy as I have, don't just believe in Him."

"Remember that no matter how old you become, that I've prayed for you. It's something that works outside of time and it spans generations Amy. My parents and grandparents prayed for me too. I can remember my Mom sitting on the front porch as I'd come home late at night, telling me she had been praying. Honey, I was once a very different person than I am now and my parent's prayers are probably the reason I'm here with you today. I am praying for my children and my grandchildren because I can't see what your life will hold, but God does."

"Amy honey, one thing you need to understand though is that prayer is not only talking to God; it's listening to Him too. Talk to him as if you're talking to your best friend. Listen and read your Bible. Learn His voice for your best friend is just what He is, and what He always will be. In this way honey, your prayers will never come to an end."

༅

Through that conversation and so many others, Dad gently and skillfully planted the seeds of faith which my heart needed to learn. He shared stories of first-hand accounts of how God answers prayer. Dad taught us about the mercies and grace of God through asking us to trace God's hand in the events of each day.

Once crippled with arthritis, my grandfather had to carry Dad. He explained how God answered the prayers of his father and the way it affected his life. God transformed him. He not only could walk, but he never suffered from arthritis again. Dad saw God move in his own life which touched his heart and affected him greatly for the rest of his days.

The accounts of faith and prayer were abundant. They shined as precious gems within the threads of each person's life through the stories Dad shared. Prayer changed and influenced the trivial to the crucial. Into this environment the birth of my uncle Earl, the evangelist, occurred but to an extent, Dad's entire family held this place for me.

My grandfather searched the scriptures to discover how current events played into prophecy. This showed his family that the word of God still is active. The Bible still speaks without question, to our daily life and throughout current events.

Orphaned by a tragedy, legacies still exist of how this shaped my great grandfather and his siblings. They had come as a family to begin a new life, in Aaron's Creek, Ohio, after their mother's passing during the birth of the youngest child. Ranging in age from a few months to late teens, they watched their father die within an hour of being run over by the horse drawn wagon.

Parceled out to strangers in the community, to whoever would take them into a home, their lives changed – permanently. Each of Dad's stories held a common theme: when our faith and strength is in God, a person can handle and overcome anything that happens. Life may never be the same but joy and hope will always come again.

Dad shared with me the precious legacies of trust and belief in

God. He demonstrated the relationship of daily interaction in the Bible and prayer. Though these things aided drawing me to God, they were not enough to save me. It helped me learn the principles of faith, but could not complete the task of surrender. That, had to be a decision I made for myself.

One Sunday evening we attended worship at our Nazarene church. On that night a movie would be shown in the sanctuary. An exceptionally rare occurrence for our church to do, this had to be an important film.

Their decision to show the movie would make an eternal difference in my life. The 1974 film called The Burning Hell was a dramatization of what it may be like if a person chooses not to serve the Lord then dies and goes to hell. To the heart of a ten year old girl, I was certain I did not want to go there. At the end of the movie, the congregation stood for prayer and I reached for Dad's arm.

"Daddy, I have to go forward. Dad, I need to be saved."

"Go on," he said smiling.

From the back row, I couldn't make it to the altar fast enough. My heart was pounding. I recognized I needed Jesus to redeem my sin. I understood I could not go to heaven simply for being good or for believing with my mind but refusing to accept this in my heart. It was all I could do not to run toward the altar.

About halfway down the aisle, though, I hesitated and looked around me. My dad had not come. He was not by my side; I was going alone. I didn't understand, and it bothered me but I continued to the altar and gave my heart to God. As we drove home following the service, I asked him why he had let me go alone. His explanation was simple, yet profound.

"Honey, I won't always be by your side. Salvation is a journey you,

alone, can make. I'm proud of you. I'm proud of your decision and I prayed with you. Just because you didn't see me, just because you didn't feel me there, does not mean I wasn't by your side."

I didn't understand that; it made no sense. This is the only memory I have of anything my dad did which hurt my heart. While that troubled me for a while, I simply tucked it away. I loved him too much to hold it against him.

The day came when I finally understood. This sting was never to wound. Instead, its cut meant skillfully to shape the person I would become as I continued to grow in life and in relationship with Christ. Dad was teaching my own walk with God is important. I could not be carried by someone else's faith. People I love may not always be by my side. I alone, can decide what my relationship with Christ becomes.

Generously planting and watering these seeds of faith through actions, prayers and lessons continued until my dad's final day. He was always helping to ensure solid foundations continued to develop while also confirming they remained steady and sure. As he aged into his nineties, he was unable to go to church and he couldn't get up and down from his knees safely to pray. His prayer time became that of only sitting in his chair. He asked two questions that made little sense.

"Is Amy ok?"

"Is he good to her?"

Over and over these questions came. We told him yes. Indeed, I was fine... then. My dad asked the questions which drove him to pray for me often. As if something were placed upon his heart which I still had yet to experience, I will always be glad he took the time to pray.

In Dad's final days, illness had caused his electrolytes to become imbalanced. We didn't realize the severity of this. He seemed to get better. On his final day, he got up, walked to the door and opened it. My mom asked *"What are you doing?"* He replied, *"I wanted to see the day."*

She helped him sit down on the sofa. He asked for a glass of water and began saying his morning prayers. This was his final conversation with his best friend. When she returned with his water, he had passed into eternity. After more than fifty years of walking with God as a Christ follower, Dad stepped into the greater life of the glory of heaven.

These experiences became precious foundations. They shaped my life. They formed the basis of my relationship with God, and would become the anchor of my faith in the moments I most needed the stability of something unshakable solidly in place.

No, it hadn't been by chance I was my father's daughter. Or that I was born at the stage of his life when he had time to devote to the instruction he wanted his children to learn. It hadn't been by coincidence I was raised in the simple, quiet place I called home. It had all been part of a beautifully divine plan to allow me to trace God's hand. An invitation to see a precious crimson thread of His love, in the good moments and through the darkness of the night seasons which would one day come. May Your Love Father become the measure of grace.

May we praise you, God
for that which draws us to pray.

Chapter 2

Gifts From God

God gives good gifts to His children. In His precious mercy, God would allow me to learn such a lovely aspect of this truth. God's favors are delightful, easy and satisfying. These gifts reflect the joyful blessings which God takes pleasure in granting.

Yet, there are gifts which may be challenging, creating distinct teachable moments for lessons of faith. There are even moments when the blessings He shares are not tangible. Instead, the present becomes that of learning the faithfulness of God, trusting in His love, seeing Him in profoundly new, deeper, and more wonderful ways because of those difficult things.

There would be one gift in my life which carried many lessons. Into that blessing God would weave intricately and delicately the picture of His mercy, and the vastness of His love into each aspect of His instruction of my heart. Love becomes the measure of grace. God would teach that faith and love often determines how our heart sees a particular gift.

༈

I had met my husband through a friend from my church. My sister and I never dated in high school. That was one thing which simply was not done by respectable young ladies, according to my dad. We did not go to dances, and it took a minor miracle for Mom to talk Dad into letting me go see Black Beauty in a movie theater. While Dad's philosophies kept his daughters sheltered in the aspect of worldly experience, they were also very protective in their nature.

Each of these teachings helped develop the ideals of love and respect that still follow his three daughters to this day. The golden rule of *"Do unto others as you would have them do unto you"* (LUKE 6:31), is a strong character trait within the heart of each of my dad's children. It also is that which will bother us the most when we see it not being done. So at times my brother-in-law has to remind us that we give so much we have a tendency to expect too much out of people.

As Dad became elderly, he needed to have someone with him when my mother went to work. My older sister, Jane, lived three hours away. Vanessa, my younger sister, had worked toward a dream of becoming a neurosurgeon since she was in middle school. That dream later changed when she met her husband. They married and moved out of state to begin a family.

I had been working on an education degree and was employed at a day care center just around the corner from my home. It was an easy decision to make. I would be the one who cared for Dad.

My mom did not drive; I took her to and from work. After dropping her off, I sometimes called to check on a friend from my church who had multiple sclerosis. A gentleman often was on the other line checking on her too. He was a *"Christian,"* took her to the grocery store, and he helped take care of her needs.

After a few times of clicking back and forth on the phone, my friend said we should just meet. He was the second person I had dated, and the only long term relationship.

Names carry meaning. Jonathan's name was significant, for it meant a gift from God. As the late afternoon sun began to set beautifully over the horizon and the cicadas made their song, there stood the man that I would eventually marry. Jonathan, was about six foot one and of average build. As an identical twin, he wore a mustache to easily distinguish himself. Jonathan's silver rimmed glasses highlighted his blue gray eyes against his black hair which had grayed slightly at his temples.

We chatted a few minutes together with our wheel chair bound friend. He asked permission for her to excuse us so he could take me to the park and buy me ice cream. The conversation was light as we traveled only a few miles to pick up vanilla cones. Afterward, we made our way to a quiet picnic area, high atop a hill, overlooking the park's small lake with its beautiful fountain. Jonathan seemed a little nervous. Jonathan fidgeted with a few twigs which he snapped from the foliage that surrounded the table and he simply spent time with me.

As the *"getting to know you"* conversation continued, we talked about the basic things and we talked about faith. No red flags stood out to alert me of any concern at all, and the evening flowed with the seamless and effortless perfection of a treasured memory in the making.

"Would you like to take a walk?" he asked. I agreed. A walk certainly seemed to be a lovely thing to do as the softness of dusk gently ushered in the preciousness of that evening.

A nice trail circled around the base of the hill, beyond the arena for the horses, where we could catch glimpses of deer. The other trail held a place where, if it had rained just enough, we would meet a little waterfall. Both held a wonderful charm, and I waited to learn which he would choose. We made our way to the lower one, beyond the softball fields and the picnic shelters. The trail passed the park maintenance office and circled farther still into the beauty of the park.

The light of the moon began to shine and with the soft serenade of the insects in the background, Jonathan reached over gently to take my hand. Along the path we walked together, enjoying the solitude of the trail. There was no need to talk, to carry on idle conversation. Instead, we had only to be, and take in the wonders of the magnificence of creation all around us. The dirt trail was smooth but marked by crushed gravel or even deep potholes in places as if, unknowingly, foretelling the journey that would lie ahead for us.

As the tree lined trail opened into a clearing he stopped, Jonathan drew me to him. He laced his hand lightly in mine and his other encircled my waist until it rested softly on the small of my back. He smiled, trying to assure that for this moment, with this small sample of his heart, I was and may forever be, held completely safe in his arms. My eyes met his and time drifted tenderly into nothingness, standing delightfully still, poised to witness the beauty which came in that first gentle kiss.

There was perfection in the wonderful simplicity of our time together. There was peacefulness in such a relaxing stroll. In the magic of the slight breeze which swept softly by and in the glow of the moment with him, in that instant, he became the magician.

Jonathan had done all the right things. He had said all the right things, all the things my heart longed to hear. In merely this one magnificent evening, I was now completely captivated by him.

The coolness of nightfall had begun to settle in, and I shivered slightly as a stronger breeze blew past us. *"I'd better be getting you home now. Would you join me again tomorrow?"* he asked as we walked back toward where he had parked.

"Yes, I believe I'd like that." I replied to him and with that, he took me back to our friend's home. After a few minutes of polite conversation he then eased an end to a most wonderful evening.

It was easy to be with him. We laughed, and we smiled. Jonathan picked me up for church and went to Bible study with me a few times. The only thing he would never do is pray with me. Though I didn't understand this, my heart did not want to question it. I was falling in love with him. I loved and trusted easily, maybe a little too easily.

When I was shy and timid, Jonathan drew me to him so I felt

comfortable. We saw each other every day. When we were apart, he called often. He was never far from my mind.

We spent an afternoon with the friend who had introduced us and enjoyed a movie together. I had chosen an old black and white movie called The Scarlet Pimpernel. Teaching us to look beneath the surface of individuals in our own lives, the film is based on a novel about an eighteenth-century English aristocrat who is much deeper than most people perceive. To those around him, the main character appears weak and ineffectual. Yet, he engages in a secret effort to free French nobles from the Reign of Terror displaying instead great strength and courage.

At one point a gentleman acquaintance of our friend came in and said, *"He's watching that and not complaining. Now that boy is in love."* Jonathan brought me flowers, bought me treats, and did all the little things which make a person feel special. He led, and I followed.

On a beautiful but cool afternoon in late autumn Jonathan took me once again to the park which had become our special place. We walked the same trail we did on that first night. We enjoyed our time together, chatting about the things which had occurred from the time we had met.

On the way back to where we parked, Jonathan stopped for a moment and picked up two clover leaves. He plucked each petal and said,

"She loves me."

"She loves me not."

"She loves me."

"She loves me not."

He then plucked only one more and said, *"She loves me."*

I smiled and said, *"She does."*

Oh! The smile that lit up his face! Jonathan left me hanging though; I had to ask *"Well, does he?"*

Jonathan grinned sheepishly and then said, *"He does."*

I had prayed for this man, who was to become my husband. In every way Jonathan was the answer to my prayers. He was my gift from God. I was totally, helplessly, completely head over heels for him and enjoying every moment we spent together.

God gives good gifts to those who ask Him. He also gives us the ability to make choices. Sometimes, the gift becomes seeing Him, as God, redeem things which may not seem good on the surface. There are times when God allows things in our life simply for His reasons and purposes.

ISAIAH 55:8-9 says it like this,

"For my thoughts are not your thoughts, neither are your ways my ways," declares the Lord. "As the heavens are higher than the earth, so are my ways higher than your ways and my thoughts than your thoughts."

Often we suppose only easy paths are God's will. We can mistakenly believe things which require effort or don't flow are not God's hand at work. This is not always the case. Lessons are sometimes formed by the acknowledgement that God's ways are not my ways. Accepting God's will in that which was beyond my understanding would form a valuable aspect to the faith God was teaching my heart. A gift from God may not always be easy. However, every gift will hold treasures of God all its own.

My family and several people from my church were not quite so fond of Jonathan. They saw flags of concern early in our relationship, of control and manipulation. A few even tried to caution me to step back and look at how he treated people. I only saw him with others when he was with me, though. Still, they were right and the day would come when it became very painful to admit and accept responsibility that I had entered into a marriage covenant with a person, against the caution of people in my life. One thing had overshadowed all their words of concern.

I loved Jonathan.

In so many ways, I simply could not see beyond that love for him. As I listened to a person share his worry, we spoke about mercy:

"Are we perfect?" I asked. "Should others not take risks on us, because of our imperfections? If we live our life unwilling to take a risk on loving another person, then we will miss what God has for us in both good and in bad. We will miss what we will learn of God, ourselves and others.

"Aren't we as Gomer to God? Didn't Hosea honor God and take Gomer to be his wife even though he suspected it may be difficult or may cost him something? Didn't God love us and take a chance on us because of His love for us even though God understood it would cost Him his Son to redeem us and should we not show mercy to others?"

Had I not chosen to marry the man I loved and believed I had been called to marry, I would not have known the many beautiful things which I held and saw in my life. I would not have experienced the most precious blessing up to this point that I have held – the gift of answered prayer and a beautiful child.

Had I not chosen to marry this man I loved, I would not have learned such amazing lessons of the faithfulness of God. He can redeem devastation, even the horrific. God is able to reshape shattered pieces of the soul into a stronger life, because it was broken.

Because of my marriage, I would need to rely on God in greater ways. In trusting Him I would come to experience His love and mercy more deeply. I chose to walk this path because I chose to honor God's leading in my heart.

We began dating in September. We were married the following June. Marriage is a beautiful thing. It is an example of how Christ loves the church. It is also a ceremony of vows. Before a Holy God, we make a life-long promise. The vows taken before God are important. They are not simply words. Two people are joined together before

God, becoming one. I agreed with and I spoke these words:

"I take you to be my husband. To have and to hold from this day for-ward, for better or worse, for richer or poorer, in sickness or in health, to love and to cherish till death us do part. According to God's holy law, this is my solemn vow."

Chapter 3

Waiting for Miracles

I wish I could say I learn the easy way, but that is not the case. For me, most often challenges, puzzles or difficulties are what help me learn best. At times, even my stubbornness can be a divine gift which God allows to draw me closer to the lesson He wants me to know. In certain circumstances, this characteristic also needs to be left at the cross in prayer, so I may willingly yield to those who lead in love.

In all things, that persistence is a gift which God recognized had to be a definitive trait within my heart. He created me with just enough determination to keep trying something until a goal can be accomplished or challenges are worked out as best as possible. There are two things that loyal perseverance says the heart can never give up on: the first is God, the second is people. God would use this tendency He created within me to show me He is God and He answers prayer.

To many, parenthood comes quite easy. Some may simply consider it's just a routine phase of life and there are also those who tragically cast children away as if life means nothing. There are still others who pray for the gift of children. At times, having a baby does not come without difficulty, or in some cases, it may not come at all.

At the age of 26 and during a routine exam, a physician felt something abnormal. The doctor was concerned enough to refer me instantly to another physician who asked questions about what I was experiencing. My answers concerned him enough to do blood work and additional tests.

I had a mass on my ovary the size of a tennis ball. The physician sent me, within the same week, to a gynecological oncologist. By the time I reached the third physician I was quite nervous, and he knew it.

I did not have cancer, but I did have surgery. The surgeon removed the mass, which turned out to be a cyst, and removed most of the ovary. Things should have been just fine, but month after month held no signs of pregnancy. I saw three or four physicians and even had an *"exploratory"* surgery before I received the diagnosis of unexplained infertility.

Short of medication and artificial means, I did everything I could to have a child. Obviously, Jonathan was involved in that process too. His desire for a child though was basically to appease me. Still, my heart wanted a child and God was designing my adventure of faith.

The Bible tells us that God can move mountains through faith. In His Holy word, story after story shares with us glimpses into the lives of individuals. The people of the Bible were just like you and me. Their flaws are highlighted and their strengths are shown. Many trusted God enough to believe the improbable, and even more accurately, to believe the impossible.

I had listened to the first-hand accounts of healing prayers that transformed lives. I believed that God could make a way where there seemed to be no way. So I began a wonderful journey to find a precious new level of faith – the faith that comes with seeing God answer prayer. Not just simply in the life of people, but specifically in my own, at the point of my need.

Our tiny little den was my favorite room. It felt so inviting with its warm knotty pine paneling. Old books and my collections filled its bookshelves. A large picture window looked out onto the backyard and up the hill, to the double row of pine trees which separated our house from the one above us. It was comforting and relaxing.

This room became a sanctuary for me and it held a different ambiance than any other in my home. I would sew, read, relax, and have my devotions. I lifted my prayers up to the Living God for a child. Here, I spent time with God and here, in some very precious moments, I even felt as if He chose to spend time with me too.

I read many times the passages of Hannah in the first and second Chapters of 1 Samuel. She, too, prayed to have a child. I read of Abraham and how God granted him a son in Genesis Chapters 18 and 21.

Then, after a long and frustrating day I sat down to have my devotions. On that quiet and rainy evening, I saw a verse I had never before noticed. By that point, I had read my Bible many times over, but this verse had never even piqued my attention until that night.

Often in devotions God will deal with areas of the heart which need His touch, wisdom, shaping, discipline or instruction. On this evening, though, it was God's love and His promise which was so pronounced to my heart. It was as if one verse stood alone on the page:

"He settles the childless woman in her home as a happy mother of children." (PSALM 113:9)

That sentence was all it took for me to believe God would change my life. I prayed God's word back to Him. I did this not so much to remind God what He had already said, but to remind myself to trust His promises, to stand in faith with the God who could do the impossible.

In one beautiful moment, faith was born in my heart that indeed, there would surely be a child. I cried tears of elation, tears of knowing God was, is and would be, faithful to His own promise. God would answer my prayers in the fullness of His time. All I had to do was wait for the miracle of the... *"one day."*

Along with this verse many others helped add to my faith. I read more of Bible characters such as Abraham:

ROMANS 4:17-18

"As it is written: 'I have made you a father of many nations.' He is our father in the sight of God, in whom he believed—the God who gives life to the dead and calls into being things that were not.

"Against all hope, Abraham in hope believed and so became the

father of many nations, just as it had been said to him, "So shall your offspring be."

I chose a name for a baby girl and for a little boy, and I prayed for that child every single night, for five years.

As I began a season of waiting, I was strong. I believed, I trusted, I did what I could, and still there was nothing. I understood that delay is not always a denial by God, but month after month showed that prayer had not yet been answered.

Discouragement filled some moments. Frustration filled other moments. Pregnancy seemed to be coming easy to others, even for those who didn't appear to value the life I so desperately wanted to carry. I wanted to hand a child back to God to say, *"This is the child You gave me Lord,"* and month after month, there was simply disappointment.

Jonathan didn't comprehend what it meant to my heart to have a child. He went along with all the efforts but he didn't pray with me. He didn't go to appointments with me and didn't understand my tears when nothing we tried was working.

Still I prayed, even through all this and even when well-intentioned Christ followers said, *"Amy, you can't do that with Scripture. You can't take them like that."* I understood their point. Yet, they had not been in my Bible study as the scripture seemed to leap off the page and into my heart.

Dad reminded me of another story of faith to help grow my strength. He shared with me a story about my grandfather, Ephraim. He also prayed for his family in the face of opposition by other well intentioned souls.

During the influenza pandemic of 1918, Papa Ephraim stood in church and testified he had prayed about this illness. He was at peace.

He felt God assured him that not only would no member of his family pass away from the illness; no one would even become sick.

After the service his pastor caught him and chastised his testimony, asking him, *"What will you do when someone in your family becomes sick?"*

Papa looked at his pastor and said, *"Pastor, I don't know about you, but I believe God."*

Ephraim Tobin had seen God answer his prayers. He had learned to listen to God's leading, and to just rest in Him. In an epidemic when millions were dying, not one member of my grandfather's family got as much as a cold that winter.

I want faith like that. I wanted it then, I still want it now. Beyond all doubt, I want to know God is always faithful to His word, His promises are sure and I want to have the faith to say even as the Hebrew children said in DANIEL 3:17-18:

"If we are thrown into the blazing furnace, the God we serve is able to deliver us from it, and he will deliver us from Your Majesty's hand. But even if he does not, we want you to know, Your Majesty, that we will not serve your gods or worship the image of gold you have set up."

Something wonderful happened over that precious season. I learned more and more to trust in God. Not superficial trust, but that which grows because I experienced God in my life.

I lifted a deeply desired, faith filled prayer up to the One who created the universe and all that exists. I learned no matter what life holds, God is always there. Instead of seeing each month as an answer of *"no,"* I viewed each month as an answer of *"not quite yet."*

Perceptions changed in my heart. My ways of viewing things were often now seen through a lens of faith. I trusted God was still preparing me to receive the child He planned for me.

How wonderful God is to share glorious lessons! Waiting on miracles meant learning to see this season as something which held a timeless and magnificent beauty all its own. It was a season of discovering the heart of God's love and faithfulness during my most difficult times!

God makes His goodness known to us along the path of life and each phase along the journey including when we wait to see God answer our prayers. There were stages of development and deepening faith. Each phase of the lesson held a richness of its own and teachings which drew me just a little deeper, just a little closer to the God I loved.

The beginning phase was only a simple request. Prayer was shallow and superficial. As my faith grew, there came deeper periods of learning to trust God more. I traced His hand more often. In doing even that one simple act of looking for God's hand, faith exploded within my heart.

Finally, I reached a point of releasing my will and my plans to that of the will of God. How sweet it is to offer back to God the dreams which He places on the heart. I yielded those growing desires as a magnificent sweet sacrifice of love lifted up to Him.

What a rich journey of faith, this time in between waiting for miracles and holding the answer held to my heart. In my humanity, I wish the answers to my prayers come in the way I choose, and in my timing. Yet, the path of faith teaches: to wait for miracles is not, simply, to wait for an answer to prayer, but to glimpse the loving hand of God in the details of the journey.

I wanted to echo in my heart the words of HEBREWS 11: 1, *"Now faith is confidence in what we hope for and assurance about what we do not see."* I didn't want *"wishing for"* faith but I wanted the faith of earnest expectation in God. Faith that knows God will be God in all things and in all ways.

I heard the testimony of a mother who experienced multiple

losses in pregnancy. She said that she was grateful God had blessed her with each one. She carried every child for a very short time before having to release the baby to God. After listening to this mother's story, I remember telling God, *"The child You will give to me is Yours. I will care for him or her as long as You choose even if one day I have to release the child back to You."*

Those words would one day become important. I don't feel I was ready until I reached that point, though really, I don't believe there was any way to be completely prepared for the journey ahead. Still, my heart had to be willing to walk its path no matter the difficulties, no matter the cost.

Until then, the answer to the prayers for which I prayed was mine. It had been something I wanted. It was a dream I held, and it was good. However, I had not reached the point that my prayer became wholly for God – for His will, for His ways, not my own to be done. I had never realized while I had been praying to Him, I was still praying for my own will to be done. I released the prayer to him as something which no longer belonged to me.

Each of the children from the story I listened to, who were conceived and returned to God without a chance to live life as we perceive it, had a gloriously defined purpose. Through their story I saw life as something that would be God's, and prayer became something for His purpose, not my own – for His glory, not solely for my own joy.

My father passed away the middle of August. The blanket of grief that shrouded my family was significant. We had peace in knowing Dad stepped into a greater life in heaven, but our hearts missed him deeply.

In the sadness of those weeks which followed I wasn't doing the normal things which go along with the science of fertility. No taking temperatures occurred, no charting or testing. There was only grief. Only emptiness existed. The only comfort to my heartache was found in God. My husband did his best to lessen my pain in the only ways he knew how. The softness of a hug, the gentleness of his hand in mine and the warmth of his love brought peace during a time when I needed it the most.

Within the month that followed Dad's passing, I became pregnant with a child. The emptiness in my heart God would fill once again and show in such a wonderful way, it is He who gives life. Before I discovered that I was pregnant I had a dream of a child. It is just a simple dream about being handed a beautiful little girl all wrapped up in a blanket and it holds a place in my heart all its own.

In so many ways God was developing my faith. There would be many complications in my pregnancy. I still waited on my miracle and to hold this answer to my prayers in my arms. In so many ways He was teaching me to trust Him no matter what my life held or the journeys I would face.

Chapter 4

Disintegration

"Thought for the day: Find God in all circumstances, even the difficult" was written on the card I received from the woman who had been assigned as my mentor at church when I was a teen. *"In your devotions search for ways that God has allowed something to shape your life because of the difficulty you experienced. Praise Him for that which draws you to pray."*

That connection, made by my pastor, has now spanned almost thirty years. Shelby Easter wasn't just a teacher. Our assignment had just been to do a weekly Bible study for 3 months. She didn't stop there, however. Shelby still calls me and we end every conversation in prayer. She has consistently reflected Christ in my life and encouraged me to look beyond the things that are temporary to find eternal value.

Those words, *"Praise Him for that which draws you to pray,"* would come to mean a great deal. We want life to be easy but this isn't always what happens. God always gives good gifts, but He sometimes allows the difficult to shape who He wants us to become in our relationship with Him.

I learned about the things that held Jonathan's interest to have things we could enjoy together. He did his best to teach me about all things electrical even though I really was not much interested in that. I tried though, for him. Jonathan tried to do the same for me. He put a sewing room together for me. As a present, he purchased a new sewing machine that did embroidery work. He then put a sitting area together for me to enjoy in my favorite room of the house.

I was happy. I felt loved. He knew the things I collected, and I often found an unexpected gift of a new Precious Moments figurine, or a Longaberger basket waiting for me. Our early days together were beautiful ones and a blessing to my heart.

Things, however, are not always as they appear. How often we as human souls hide behind masks! I would learn that just because someone acts one way when they are trying to win your heart, it may not always carry over completely as truth.

I did not have a perfect marriage; no marriage is perfect. Every marriage is flawed with at least one significant issue. Each husband and wife is a human being, with all their gifts and talents but also with all their weaknesses.

I make many mistakes. Often I fail. At times I can be stubborn, and I struggle with sin as much as Jonathan did. Still, I loved him though. There are also moments when I believe that down deep, he really did love me. Nevertheless, as our marriage progressed, it seemed as if he had a harder and harder time showing that love.

"Praise Him for that which draws you to pray." It's on our knees where transformation begins. Life isn't always easy. I prayed for Jonathan and pleaded for God to help our marriage. I asked God to transform me into a reflection of Him toward my relationship with Jonathan and others. I made a decision to love even in the difficult things. I prayed many things and sometimes, I just cried. I asked that I would trust God no matter what my life held. I wasn't just trusting Jonathan. I was trusting God.

Choices are always with us. Faith, hope and love are decisions we make. They will leap over our barriers, they will tear down our walls and they will make the impossible – possible. I loved Jonathan. I would also learn that love is not always enough to reach the unreachable depths of a soul. That, is held by God alone. Even in those things which would bring great pain, my heart had two questions that faith would need to answer.

What makes a soul cling so deeply to God?
What is there which makes the unbelievable, truth?

While testimonies are important and can both bring glory to God as well as help others, we must also remember that people are human. There are many who deal daily with the impact of Jonathan's actions. It's important in telling the story of God's love and grace that we also remember to give as much mercy as possible to those who didn't know the full depth of the things occurring in our home. In the highest respect, we'll see only short glances into the window of our home.

At times the gift to my heart was not necessarily the husband for whom I had prayed, but the God who faithfully walked with me in difficult moments. Our marriage progressed with Jonathan becoming increasingly controlling and violent when angry. I was sleeping and one night got up to use the rest room. He sat up in bed and he back handed me across the face scratching my eye with his finger nail. As one may imagine, doing my best to cover up what had occurred made for a few difficult conversations for several days following that incident as my eye healed.

As the days turned into years, it became progressively more difficult for Jonathan to hold down steady employment. My salary was direct deposited, and I had no control over the finances in our household. Jonathan required me to ask to go out to lunch, to buy a pack of gum, and there would be a moment when he would force me to beg, on my knees, for enough gasoline to drive to work. On that day, however, he proudly showed me a new $150.00 ham radio. I didn't mind what Jonathan purchased at all. Those things made him happy and even intrigued me. What bothered me was that he hadn't talked with me, especially, when he made such a big deal about me asking him to do anything.

I was irritated, and I told him so, adding, *"How much more should you have discussed this with me when you want me to ask you before I do anything and you know it's my money you were spending?"*

"Is it?" He retorted. *"You married me. It's our money. I am the head of this family, Amy Elisabeth, not you, and as such I don't need to explain anything at all to you. Your only role is to do what I tell you."*

Then in typical Jonathan fashion he diverted attention from his actions to turn things around to my fault. He said, *"Amy Elisabeth, should we even be having this discussion right now? You know your place. How would Christ look at your behavior? When you know the Bible says, 'Wives submit to your husbands.' Your attitude is definitely not being submissive right now. And you say you want to be a godly woman,"* he said with sarcasm. *"You sure will never be one, acting like this."*

I can't say I reflected Christ well through giving a gentle and soft answer in my response to him. I said, *"Because I pointed out you did something behind my back when you make me ask you about everything I do? Seriously? And you said that godly woman part, Jonathan, just to hurt me because you know I really do want to be."*

I continued, *"So ok, let me ask you a few questions then, my dear Jonathan, if you're the head of this family, shouldn't you be working? And since you're the one who went to the submission thing – as my husband don't you know how you're supposed to lead me? You say things to deliberately hurt me, you don't pray with me, you don't go to church with me any longer, you don't read the Bible with me but yet you sure like to use it against me a lot. If you'd actually pick up and read the book you're putting me in my place with, you'd see that's not exactly how things go. The Chapter about submission is about walking in the way of love and goes on to say 'Husbands love your wives even as Christ loved the church and gave himself up for her' (EPH 5: 25). So why not give that a try for a change and I bet you'll find out I'll be more than happy to submit to you.... whenever you love me."*

Oh! Wow, that made him mad! He rushed at me. He grabbed

my throat, shoved me out of the room into the hallway, up against the wall of the staircase and squeezed until I could not take a breath. Those few moments felt like an eternity as I struggled to pry his hand off my throat. The more I struggled the harder he tightened his grip – until I couldn't struggle any further. Then he said, *"What is it you would like to tell me now?"* I mouthed, *"I'm sorry. I can't breathe."* Then he let me fall to the floor.

I called the police only once in my twelve year marriage. I loved my husband. He was a human soul with wonderful qualities and yet, he could also be a very different person when he was angry. There was a public persona he kept to acquaintances and to look at him one would have thought of an attractive man and a loving husband. At times, this was absolutely correct.

Behind the closed doors of my home, as in so many others, there lurked within the silence a demon that could engulf the soul. Abuse has no barriers. It crosses all cultures, it's seen in all income levels, and strikes in every denomination as well as every profession. It can be hidden by strength and position. It can be hidden by fear. It can be tucked away from questions through increasing isolation, and can be hidden from view through a well-placed sleeve of a blouse. It can even be disguised in the realm of dutiful submissiveness. No, not every difficult relationship is abuse. When it is present, however, it is frightening, dangerous and deadly.

As with most true victims of abuse I have no evidence to substantiate the things I share with you here. In fact, Jonathan went to great lengths to protect himself should I attempt to ever reveal the things in our home. He recorded some of my *"emotional outbursts"* without my permission while he never taped the things leading up to my tears. Then, Jonathan would tell me he loved me. This is called a manipulative cycle and it's seen in most cases of abuse.

In my home the cycle went something like this. An act of violence occurred. Then, there were periods of calm when Jonathan felt in control of our home, was repentant and even promised to change. It was the tranquil times which reminded me why I fell in love with him. This gave me the hope my prayers were being answered, transformation could occur, the abuse would stop, and these things kept me in the relationship.

I truly loved my husband, as with most victims of abuse. The victim is told by the perpetrator, and so comes to believe, that it's our fault. I was told I was the reason he had to hit me. I simply had to do what I was told and things would be fine. I was also cautioned that if I left, I would be harmed or I would never make it on my own.

This pattern has a triple effect: the threats and violence frighten, and as the *"it's your fault"* begins to take hold and the victim accepts responsibility, it enables the abuser to feel justified in continuing their behavior. As the periods of calm then come, the victim hopes that they can change the situation and can limit the abuse and finally stop it.

In my situation, as is true in most, change did not occur.

Chapter 5

Beholding Miracles

What is it about the time in between the answer of prayer and holding that answer in your arms that becomes so special, so holy to a heart? It is deeply poignant to see how often the God of all creation seems tenderly to draw those who follow Him to come even a little closer, to know Him still more. With a heart of love, He asks us to look far beyond the gift, to Him as the One who offered it.

God teaches so gently, especially in the midst of things which contain concern or heartache. The time in between for me held a season of complications to the pregnancy. In this phase, I would learn new lessons. God would never ask me to set aside the reality of what I experienced; He would only ask my heart to allow Him to be God in the middle of them.

He never asks us to deny the human emotion which makes us a living soul. Instead, God asks each of us to give those emotions of the heart back to Him. Oh, how these simple truths are seen again and again. Each time, they beautifully bring the blessing of learning more deeply, the love of God.

This pregnancy which was the answer to so many years of prayer was plagued with significant problems. I had morning sickness so badly that I lost 25 pounds before it stopped. When I began bleeding it went immediately into a high risk status. I was placed on bed rest and there were nights I would lay awake and just pray for this answer to prayer growing in my womb.

A beautiful, precious life of a little girl was growing inside me.

We visited the physician's office three times a week. Hospitalized four times in the course of the pregnancy and going into preterm labor once, I learned that the answer to prayer may not always be an easy thing.

I prayed so many times variations of the same basic prayer:

"God bless you Elisabeth Grace and keep you. May the Lord make His face shine on you and be gracious to you. May the Lord turn His face toward you and give you peace. Your life has been given by the Most High God, you are an answer to prayer, and may your heart always be His.

"May the gifts that God has placed within you grow, and be offered back up to Him. May all that God desires for you be completed. May no weapon ever formed against you prosper. By faith, I speak blessing and life to you. Elisabeth, you will live and not die and declare the glory of God. May the Lord Himself fight your battles, and may you dwell in the house of the Lord forever."

After the status changed to high risk, the physicians would ask me to call if there was anything unusual. Then they brought me in to be checked. One morning, I went in because I was spotting and after an exam, I was quickly flipped up with my legs higher than my head and wheeled into labor and delivery.

The staff from NICU came in to speak with me. The nurse explained all that could potentially happen if the baby was born at that point. The complications to a pre-term birth are never good, and I prayed.

It would be easy to dismiss pre-term labor as yet another complication of the pregnancy but I was given a medication to develop the baby's lungs. On the day Elisabeth Grace did draw her first breath, I would come to believe and will hold in my heart until my very last breath that instead of an obstacle to pregnancy that the preterm labor situation was God's hand on her life, even in that moment.

God knows always, the end from the beginning.

My season of pregnancy was hard. My heart sometimes felt over-whelmed; I was doing all that I could for the child I carried and wor-ried it just was not enough. Now, I understood why it took prayer for me to become pregnant. Thanking God for allowing this journey, that showed me His protection over my life, I asked for His continued help for this little life and for me.

This experience taught me that God may not grant the prayer for a child simply because He may be protecting the mother from sit-uations her body may not have been able to bear. I prayed for all the other ladies who would long to have a child and may never hold it. God was being merciful to me.

I asked God to protect this precious child. In facing one issue after another with the pregnancy my heart felt that Satan, the enemy of both her soul and mine, desired to steal Elisabeth, kill her, and destroy my heart. I asked God to guard His purposes for Elisabeth and her life for Him. In tracing God's hand for her life, I searched for His blessings in my own.

Jonathan worked a part time job at a local pizza place to make up for the hours I was losing at work. He then took a position an hour away. He worked nights and would sleep during the day. There was little for me to do on the frequent periods of bed rest but lie there, counting the number of cracks in the ceiling or pray. The season was filled with concern for the baby I carried in my womb, but it was also a beautiful time of praying blessings over her life. What a wonderful time of praising God for who she was then, and who she would even-tually become.

I yielded Elisabeth Grace back up to God. She was His. With-out God answering prayer, she would not be growing in my womb. I blessed her infancy, her childhood, her teenage years and her adult-hood. I blessed her gifts and the talents which the Lord had already given her. I prayed that when Elisabeth became a mother that her pregnancy would be an easy one and she would not have to experience the things that had been issues in mine. I prayed Elisabeth would always walk with the God who had given her life and she would always know she was loved.

Jonathan only went to two appointments with me, when we found out what we were having and when the physician specializing in high risk pregnancies explained what we faced. The appointments which the baby and I had typically would go something like this. First, I would travel in the opposite direction from the hospital to pick my mom up and take her with me. Then we would make our way to the hospital, which held the physician's office, for an ultrasound one day, a checkup another day and a fetal non stress test the third day.

After a few weeks, there reached a point that this very pregnant mother practically did a happy dance on the rare occasions we could take care of both the non-stress test and the office appointment the same day. I drank soda to help Elisabeth pass her counts and then she would not move the next day. This again was God's hand of faithfulness to this unborn child but I did not know it.

I didn't feel any movement at all for so long. I enjoyed sitting in Elisabeth's nursery in a rocking chair. As I would begin gently to rock and sing, Elisabeth would wake up, motions would begin and she swiveled and kicked. I made up the words to a song. It was a simple song with a simple melody but it was our song:

"I love you. Yes, I really do.
I love you more than the sun and moon.
I love you more than all the sand
on every single sea shore around the whole land"
and I would end it with a cheery

"That's a lot of sand baby!"

Those special moments we shared will always be carried with me. They bring a smile all their own. How I loved this child! How I so very dearly loved this sweet precious child who was the answer to my prayers!

Faith was no longer the treasured stories of bygone eras. God answered prayer in my own life, for a weak and flawed individual. I saw God's hand so clearly and it changed my heart. The standing stones of faith which my dad had used to mark the way were the same rocks of faith that would carry my relationship with God to an even deeper level. God works in my life through difficult struggles and beautiful blessing.

Miracles change us.

On Friday, the beginning of Memorial Day weekend, I had one last ultrasound. I held the answer to my prayers in the daughter I carried in my womb but it had not been an easy journey and we weren't out of the woods yet. The staff sent me immediately to the physician. My chipper, *"Hi Doc, can we have this baby today?"* usually drew a chuckle. On that day, he didn't even let me ask. He said two words: *"Go upstairs."* I walked to the end of the hallway, stood at the windows on the third floor, called Jonathan and said, *"We're having a baby today! They are admitting me."*

I don't know how long I had been in the room when Jonathan and Mom arrived. They had begun to induce labor but stopped it an hour and a half later. I felt sick fairly quickly. I lay in the hospital bed on my left side and was not allowed to turn over. I still tried, and every time I did a nurse would come in and turn me back over and I drifted in and out of sleep for the rest of the afternoon.

I lay there for six hours, barely opening my eyes. Every sound was magnified terribly. Even Jonathan's voice hurt to hear.

"Jonathan I don't feel good. Could you please be quiet?" I asked as he chattered away. He kept talking.

"Jonathan, please, could you be quiet?" He didn't seem to recognize my request.

The nurse emphatically said, *"Your wife is in distress. She's asked you twice to be quiet and you haven't listened. If she has to ask you to be quiet one more time, I'll call security and you will be escorted from the hospital."*

She left the room, and he got upset. *"No one is going to make me leave,"* he began. *"I have every right to be here and no one can make me go."*

At that point, I didn't say anything else. I was too sick to fuss any further about the noise. I didn't need the nurse or security creating a stir trying to make him leave and I really didn't need him angry. I just wanted to hold my precious little baby.

At one point a different physician came into the room. He said that he had been in clinic and passed the nurses station when he saw what was taking place. He explained that I needed to have an emergency C-section or I would lose my baby.

They wheeled me to the operating room, and a nurse asked me what I was having done. All I could think was, *"If you don't know what we're having done, we are in big trouble."*

I answered their questions as the anesthesiologist came in and was seated. He sat at my head and talked to me the whole time. The surgeon was missing his daughter's dance recital to save my daughter's life.

Then the room became a commotion.

"Get NICU in here, now," the doctor said. Within seconds several people came. *"Mom, it's a girl,"* he said as he turned his back to me. He

handed her off to another person but I couldn't see her. *"Why isn't she crying?"* I asked. The physician didn't answer me. The anesthesiologist patted my arm and said, *"It's ok, they have NICU over there and they are working with her. It's going to be ok"*.

When I finally did hear Elisabeth cry my relief was apparent, especially to the anesthesiologist. You see, he was the only one talking to me. The nurse was talking to the physician. All that my husband had said to me was, *"It looks like they are lifting your stomach up with a crowbar."*

They wrapped Elisabeth up in a blanket and showed me her face. *"Here is your baby girl Mom. We are taking her to NICU. You'll be able to see her later,"* a gowned woman told me. I didn't get to hold her until the next morning.

Elisabeth would spend one week in the NICU. I could only see her during visiting hours. The rest of the time I spent alone in my hospital room. Even though hospitals give new parents a good meal when a baby is born, I had to call and beg Jonathan to come.

Jonathan's lack of involvement and his feelings for us could be summed up in what he said following the meal, *"I need to get home to my dog now. Baxter will be lonely and needs me. If anything happens to us Amy, I want you to have the baby,"* and then he quickly left.

The cord had been wrapped around Elisabeth's neck three times. Her Apgar score was one immediately after birth, and then increased to six. An Apgar score of zero is a dead baby. All Elisabeth had at the moment of birth was a heartbeat and that was weak. My placenta had three clots in it.

God had, and was, protecting this beautiful child of answered prayer and I beheld my sweet baby girl – my very precious miracle.

Your faithfulness and mercies forever abide,
we trust in You Jehovah-Ahavah, The Lord is love.

Chapter 6

Blessings

Oh the blessings of answered prayer!

Every single day I held in my arms a living and breathing miracle. For five years I prayed for a child. For five years I called this child by name and prayed for anything and everything I could conceive her life may hold. Without hesitation my heart believed beyond any doubt that God was faithful to His word.

How I had grown to trust in God over those precious days with her, and how amazingly blessed I felt to be Elisabeth's mother. Thrilled to be finally holding her in my arms I lavished love on her with cuddles and kisses. At only five pounds, she was so small that nothing I had purchased for her fit. The preemie sizes were what she needed, and that is just what my baby girl received.

The physicians told me I couldn't nurse her and Elisabeth was relegated to formula. She did not tolerate it well though. There were moments when my heart ached for her. She was connected to wires for the apnea monitor, she was not tolerating formula, and then bless her heart, she got colic. I could not fix her pain easily. I would walk around the house singing to her. The motion seemed to ease a small amount of her discomfort.

There were times I walked all night long. Elisabeth and I got in our exercise. I loved on my sweet little Elisabeth and I enjoyed her cuddles. After about a week I called my mom and cried. I had prayed for this child. I loved her so much. Nothing I was trying to do helped Elisabeth much and I would learn to trust God in new ways. But first, Elisabeth's momma really needed just a few hours of sleep!

Especially comical, Elisabeth even made herself laugh. She had a few favorite things, especially her pacifiers, and she was a little protective of those treasures of hers. She had a special place for the cup of them we kept for her and that's where she liked them to stay!

One *"pacie"* was simply not enough though. She always kept three. Elisabeth liked one in her mouth, and one in each hand. When someone asked, *"Why so many?"* I would giggle and respond, *"Well you know, just in case she had to switch one out for any reason, she's always got a couple of spares."*

She liked to squeeze the rubber part. The only time she dropped one was when she picked something up or when she drifted off to sleep and in that case, she wanted to hold my bottom lip. A few times I thought this precious child was doing her best to pull it off my face, she enjoyed it so much. I gently nibbled on her fingers and she would giggle and then settle down, nestle in on my shoulder and drift off to sleep as I rocked her.

Maw Maw Sarah and her Care Bears were among her favorite things. Elisabeth also had a favorite movie. I think we saw the movie *"Toy Story 2"* until the child could recite almost every line in it. Woody and Jesse were her most beloved dolls. She adored them, and I absolutely adored seeing her get such a thrill out of it all.

This lovable, precious answer to my prayers had a heart that so sweetly shined. Her laugh was absolutely infectious. She searched for ways to bring joy to a person's heart. Whether in simply being with her, or with something she would do or say, once she found that little spark that made a person smile she would continue it. We often heard her say, *"Now honey, you know that you are just the sweetest thing around – better than strawberry pie on a warm summer day."* Happiness filled the hearts of her family and friends. Elisabeth absolutely loved to simply love on other people.

Elisabeth was a bit mischievous as well. She liked treasure hunts, so she'd create them – usually with the things that were used most often. For instance, *"Oh, so you're looking for the remote are ya Momma? Well, if it's a treasure that you're seeking, where do you think we'll find it?"* Then she'd giggle as she watched me try to find where she had hidden the *"king's golden bounty."*

I could have called her middle name Joy for it was a prominent personality trait. She was an active little girl who was so eager to please. If Elisabeth happened to get into trouble and was scolded, she would pout, not because she was angry at being fussed at but because she so wanted to please the ones she loved.

Our time outdoors was always filled with new wonders to take in and behold. Elisabeth liked to run up to the top of the hill behind our home and then roll down, laughing as she rolled to the bottom and climb up once again. She enjoyed the wonders of simple pleasures, finding the beauty in birds and flowers and most importantly, people. Though at times she could be shy, I don't think she met many strangers. For the most part, as long as I was near she would be quite chatty and leave them by saying a cheery, *"Bye friend!"*

Elisabeth loved horses. At three, she began riding lessons and took to it exceptionally well. She had natural talent and the pony she rode was a great *"kid broke"* older mare. With a strong determination to conquer the challenge of an animal she only came up to a knee on, Elisabeth grabbed the reigns. With her trainer right beside Elisabeth, her Dora the Explorer bike helmet atop her head, she guided Star, the chestnut pony, around the training ring.

I observed from a short distance, just behind the stalls so I could see but avoid distracting her, enabling them to develop a bond. I got Elisabeth a miniature horse which was born the day she began to ride. She named him Jack. In October, Elisabeth participated in her first horse show. While she was too young and inexperienced to do a walk around on a horse, my baby girl beamed when she won not just one trophy but two for the stick horse competition. She smiled for days and those trophies were part of her *"treasures."*

I came ever so close and regret not purchasing a beautiful palomino pony called *"Honey Pie"* for her. I could look into the horse's eyes, and it was so gentle. Elisabeth loved it and so did her mother. Her father did not agree. After a very clear reminder by him, her father's stance prevailed.

This particular gift for Elisabeth was never to be, but we still shared the moment in loving on Jack and Star for a while. The times Elisabeth and I shared with horses are a beautiful and priceless memory for my heart. From the simple toys she played with every day, to the ones which she rode and loved, this brought such joy to Elisabeth's heart. I beheld her smile and sharing it with her brought such absolute pleasure to my heart and soul.

By holding Elisabeth in my arms every day as she grew, I was growing too. I was seeing things in new ways, understanding things from new perspectives because of her influence on my life. Again and again I would come back to the realizations that because of this beautiful and precious child, I experienced beyond any doubt whatsoever that God both hears and answers prayer.

Even in my inadequacies and humanity, God answers prayer and my faith in Him was off the charts. He had done the impossible in my life and I loved Him so much for it. I used to say that God gave me Elisabeth's heart to *"hang the moon."*

I smiled so much because of Elisabeth Grace.

In just about every drawing she did, Elisabeth would draw a heart. Inside that heart she would write the words *"I love you."* Over and over again I would find them – in my purse, in notebooks, on post it notes.

These precious hand-drawn hearts of hers were all over the place.

Hearts became a wonderful thing we shared together. She once got me a transparent little pink glass heart. She said, *"I love you Momma. This is like your heart Momma. Your heart shines. It has windows and you can see through it."*

Elisabeth loved to climb trees. Much to the dismay of the other parents, she taught her friends to climb them too. Not just climb them, but also hang upside down and pretend to be monkeys. There were many times when a child in a tree would say, *"Hey, look what Elisabeth taught me!"* Oh how I simply enjoyed plucking children out of trees!

One weekend the company I worked for gave us tickets to the water park. Elisabeth and I spent a wonderful day there. She loved it. She asked to go down one of the water slides. We waited in line, on the stairs of the platform which led to the top. Elisabeth knew her mother had taken a few spills and developed a healthy and thus protective fear of heights.

At seven years old, on the steps of a platform overlooking the tree tops, this beautiful little gift to my heart looked up at me, patted my arm and said, *"It's ok Momma. It's ok. You're gonna be just fine."* Then she turned, looked up at the people all around us and said, *"That's my Momma, and she doesn't like heights."* Everyone smiled, laughed and then one person replied to her, *"You are taking really good care of your Momma"* and Elisabeth just beamed! She was such a beautiful treasure in so many special ways.

Elisabeth was also learning how to cross stitch. I sat on the big green sofa to sew. Elisabeth curled beside me and said, *"Teach me Momma, teach me!"* With her beautiful brown eyes she'd look at me and ask as we stitched, *"How do you know where to put the needle at Momma?"* Then, I taught her how to follow a pattern for the design.

With such care, and the determination to learn, she took the needle in her tiny little hand and pulled it up one hole of the cream colored fabric and back through another hole, taking her time to get everything just right. *"Is this how Momma?"* she asked. Of course she got it right. She worked in the areas of the design where there was a failsafe measure of success for her. She could see her work was making a beautiful difference in the design we were stitching together and this brought her so much joy.

The laughter and love I shared with Elisabeth was so amazingly blessed. I enjoyed taking her to church and reading the Bible with her. We talked about the same stories of faith that my Dad shared with me. She was becoming a beautiful person, both in aspects of her life as a sweet, precocious little girl and as she learned more and more about God.

Oh! The wonderful fun we had together as we simply relished each other! She liked to sing *"Jesus Loves Me"* and there was one point in the chorus when our voices made a warble sound together that tickled her so much. Over and over again she wanted to sing that same spot and each time she giggled hilariously.

Elisabeth sang to me one evening, the same song I had made up just for her when I was pregnant, and sang to her so often when I rocked her to sleep. Oh, what a moment that was for my heart to hear her sing back to me:

"I love you. Yes, I really do.
I love you more than the sun and moon.
I love you more than all the sand
on every single sea shore around the whole land."
Then Elisabeth ended it with,
"That's a lot of sand Momma."

She liked to curl up on my lap and snuggle with me. Sometimes Elisabeth would turn and place her tiny little hands on my cheeks, stroke them softly and say, *"I love you my Mommy."* Sometimes she would run her fingers under my chin and say, *"Momma I'm proud of you."* She had such a loving heart.

At times when I was cleaning or doing laundry, I'd pass by her room. She would be sitting on the floor praying, out loud for others, by name. She was six and seven years old when she was doing this and it made me almost burst into joy for the heart of this beautiful, precious child. She would even look at me and say, *"Momma, that person takes care of other people but no one takes care of them, so I will. Momma, you need to tell that person we love them."* Such discernment and love from a precious little child!

Sometimes, Elisabeth would even pick violets from the yard and leave them on a chair or table for an elderly neighbor next door to find. *"How I loved to open my door to find a bouquet of violets on the table by my chair. It always made me smile, and I knew Elisabeth had been here,"* she would tell me. Elisabeth also liked to create gift baskets for people she thought did not get many gifts.

As my sweet little Elisabeth grew, her favorite songs became the Christian songs we would listen to on the radio. She would sing the songs and sometimes would ask about the meaning of the words. They became teachable moments we'd share as we simply drove around town.

Elisabeth's favorite song had become *"Finally Home"* by the group Mercy Me. She loved the melody, the opening part to it and the words. I listened to her sing and when the song finished she would say, *"Back it up Momma, back it up."* I set the CD to repeat for her and Elisabeth would sing *"when I finally make it home"* over and over again. I wondered why she picked a song about heaven as her favorite but I simply tucked this away in my heart.

PART TWO

May the light of God's love
lead us always through
the valleys.

Chapter 7

Nearing the Gate

I have passed by thousands and had never considered them before at all, these simple things called gates. It amazes me how God can lovingly teach me about Himself in the simplest things. I would learn a concept and be confronted with questions I had not really considered before as I enjoyed a nice stroll one beautiful spring morning.

There is a quiet lake surrounded by hills of pine trees. Its trails lead deep into the stillness of the surrounding forest. Its intersection of John's Creek and Aaron's Creek led me beautifully to the place time drifts back, to the stories of long ago. Here, the home built by my grandfather and great grandfather still stand, the family cemetery sits just over the crest of the hill, and stories come alive.

The land which has been in our family for generations is now in the depths of a national forest. I can walk here for hours simply basking in the beauty. As I followed the trails that crisp morning, the splendor of spring filled the forest land with the singing of birds. The breeze rustled gently through the trees.

Along the routes which lead away from the lake, I stepped off the main pathway. I made my way deeper into the stillness, into the far reaches of the trails. As I neared the edge of the forest, there was just an old simple fence and a gate that marked the passage from public land to private.

How many times had God placed fences to protect and shield me from that which lay on the other side of the wall? How many times had God opened the gate for change to take place in my life? Do I unknowingly stand on one side of the fence afraid to step through the gate into that which God offers before me? If God has placed the barrier and someone chooses by free will to open a locked gate, how will God respond?

These are such thought provoking questions for a simple stroll and time of worship with God. Still, I love the fact that His threads of love are always weaving in even the smallest of ways, always teaching through the journeys of the everyday.

My husband, daughter and I moved to the Midwest. We came for a funeral and on the trip home my husband advised we were moving. There was no discussion.

Jonathan had made his decision. He dropped me off at our house, packed clothes for himself and our daughter and left the next day, taking her with him. I spent the following three months putting all which was needed in place to leave a job that I was going to retire from, settle details regarding the house, belongings and family and traveling to this new town on weekends.

In this new area, charming small farms dot the landscape. There were no majestic mountains, no rugged terrain or whitewater rapids but there were wide open spaces. A historic and quaint little village perched majestically on the banks of a beautiful Ohio River, and a bustling metropolitan city just a few moments away, hinted of a place where wonderful new adventures just waited to become the memories of old.

On my first visit to the quiet little town where my husband had chosen for us to settle, the acres of farmland along the highways had not yet been tilled. Acres bloomed with the bright yellow of goldenrod and for a weed, it was absolutely beautiful. Jonathan had promised, *"Things would be different in this place."*

He promised many things. Elisabeth could have a horse, too, if she wanted. Elisabeth would have better schools, there would be more opportunities for her here than back home and she would grow in so many areas. There would be new things for us to do. He would go to church with us. Yes, things would be better here. All of this was what he promised.

Jonathan packed up his things and some things for Elisabeth and left me behind, alone. My heart broke and with my little Elisabeth gone, there was no question what I would do; I would go. So many people told me, *"He took Elisabeth to ensure you would come."* They were right. None of my family wanted the move to occur. They were very concerned. Still, my daughter was in the Midwest. I had to go. I simply had to settle this move in my heart and look at the positives it could hold.

I sat at the desk with my supervisor before I left, talking about the move. He said, *"Amy, I feel God has something for you there. It may even be completely different from what you are doing now, but I believe that God has something for you."* I'm a flawed individual, but since I had to go to a new place I chose to see it as a place with new opportunities ahead. I longed to serve God in a way I never did before and come to know Him so much more. I felt this would ultimately turn the move into something beautiful and positive.

In many ways, eyes are the windows to the soul. As our marriage progressed Jonathan's eyes told his own story. Where there was once peace, it had faded away. Where there was once safety, it no longer existed. Where there was once love, it was no more.

There were moments that Jonathan could be incredibly compassionate and loving, but other moments the things he would do and say made very little sense. It is hard for another person to comprehend that which can be seen during an individual's descent into the irrational. The stories of illogical thought are often difficult to explain, and in compassion, better left between the person and his God. There was little I could do to influence things in a positive way.

As the decline in our home progressed, church was not a place that Elisabeth's father wanted to be any longer. Jonathan went each week when we dated. Occasionally he attended Bible Study with me as well but he stopped completely once we were married.

Elisabeth began to realize something as we went to church. *"Momma, the other kids' Daddies take them to church, but Momma why doesn't my Daddy take me to church? Why doesn't he go with us?"* It was a hard question to answer for her so I simply said, *"Honey, we'll just have to pray and you can ask him to go if you wish."* Elisabeth had given her heart and life to God when she was in Kindergarten shortly before we moved to the Midwest.

My joy had become Elisabeth. She was my world. She was the light of my life as things disintegrated from a home of peace and blessing into a battleground of fear and pain. I truly learned how the eyes can indeed tell a story words may not be able to share.

The beauty of days we spent together journeyed on, yet we were nearing a gate we did not realize. It was one of significant change. On the other side of the gate and beyond this wall of protection which surrounded my life, our life, there would be the darkness of a night season which would attempt to engulf my soul.

Those simple stories I grew up with reminded me so clearly of faith, but also that my life is just a wisp compared to eternity. Time moves on, but there was a day when God understood my heart needed to step back and revisit that which had been before, as if to realize that though all things will fade, the memories will exist for a lifetime.

We had come to a new place. A new beginning awaited us. After completing the tasks back east, I was ready to be with my family. Once settled in at our new home, I applied for and accepted a part time position at a Christian company. Jonathan did not say a word about the application. He even drove me to the office for the interview, but he was not happy at all when I chose to accept the job.

My husband was disintegrating from the inside out. I just did not grasp how much. It had taken me three months to settle everything and complete the move. I had been here only one week when Jonathan stood in the living room of the house he had rented for us with its dark paneled walls and gold carpeting and announced that we were moving back to where we lived before.

"We came out here, we tried it and we are leaving," he told me.

Elisabeth sat in a rocker glider, her Veggie Tales movie playing on the television. I stood in the doorway to the kitchen preparing lunch when for one of the few times in my marriage I told Jonathan, *"No."*

I told him, *"I left a great job, my family and all my friends to come out here with you and I'm not going to leave after only one week just because you changed your mind. I'm happy. I'm finally doing something for God and we are staying!"*

After this, Jonathan took out his wallet and took out a concealed carry weapons permit. He shoved it in my face and said, *"You see this... this is god."* I was shaking as I looked him in the eye and said, *"That may be your god, but it is not mine and as for me and my house we will serve the Lord."*

I don't often speak of the emotions during that time. Looking back at it, I have come to both feel and believe that in some way God removed His hand from my husband that day. This man was my husband. He went to church when we were dating and called himself a *"Christian."* However, this man also stood in our home time and time again shaking his fist at the ceiling shouting *"I curse you God"* and he had now verbally declared a concealed carry weapons permit *"god."*

Jonathan then very coldly said, *"Fine, you can stay here but I'm leaving,"* and he did. He used my mother's address to declare residency by getting a driver's license in the state we just left. He would be back, however, and move us yet again to a third state in only three months.

That state was just across the river and I would find out later that he moved us there simply because of the differences in concealed carry weapons permit regulations. Jonathan was now living his life around a gun. I tried to honor my husband and save my marriage in going, but this was not a wise decision. Things would become increasingly worse and much more dangerous.

I had no way to depend on Jonathan. I had no way of knowing what was going to happen tomorrow and no way of knowing if he would stay or leave. There was no consistency. My employers took me from part time to full time so I would have a steady, stable income. They walked through the next several months with me.

Jonathan had taken out a $250,000 life insurance policy on me a few months before we moved. One day he came in to the bedroom as Elisabeth and I were reading a book together and with a sneer said, *"If anything ever happens to you, I'm going to be rich."* Then he turned and left the room. I cancelled my life insurance the next day with that company and set up another policy with Elisabeth as beneficiary and an outside source as a trustee just in case. Yes, indeed it seemed I was doing all I could to save a marriage that truly was no longer safe.

One afternoon Elisabeth came in the living room and said, *"Momma, I remember Daddy hitting you so many times you fell into the refrigerator."* That happened when she was three. She was six when she told me.

On that day I was being hit repeatedly until I fell into the edge of the refrigerator door and I needed help. I ran to the phone and dialed 911. As I did, Jonathan ripped the phone out of the wall.

The only reason the police came was because they heard Elisabeth crying in those split seconds before he tore out the phone. The officers spoke with Jonathan. Whatever they told him, after the police left Jonathan looked at me and said, *"You had better never do that again or you will regret it."* He meant it. I was afraid. And I never did.

In true cases of abuse it is especially dangerous for a person to make that call because of the possible repercussions after the police leave. Following this, Jonathan began to say, *"If you leave you'll die old and alone and no one will ever love you again."* Then with a frightening tone to his voice, he progressed on to saying an incredibly chilling phrase when he was angry with me. *"I promise you, if you ever leave you won't have Elisabeth, so you better think very seriously about your actions."*

That is something that terrifies a mother. I was afraid. What could I do? Did he really mean this? What would happen if I did leave? He has never hurt her, so is he actually saying he'll kill me? But I love him, so maybe it's just me. If I just try harder, do better, don't make him angry everything will be all right. So like most people in this situation, I stayed.

The time had now come, however, when I would have to protect Elisabeth. I would have no other choice but to try to free us. What was I teaching her about what is acceptable in the way men treat women? Would this repeat itself in her relationships one day? What would happen as she grew old enough to tell Jonathan *"No"*? Would he treat her the same as he did me?

He slept in a twin size bed with her with a loaded gun beside him on the table. He was not sleeping with me and he wouldn't let Elisabeth sleep with me. While she told me he never touched her obviously I was concerned about what could potentially occur as she grew older. I loved my daughter so even if it cost my life I would walk the journey to free us. I would protect her.

Once I had made the clear determination that for Elisabeth's safety and my own, we could no longer stay with Jonathan, leaving would not be as easy as it sounded. I sat in the swing outside the little white rented house in the cool of an early autumn evening as Elisabeth laughed and played. She was riding her bike with the children in the neighborhood. Jonathan came out the front screen door, walked off the porch down the two concrete stairs, over to the swing and sat down beside me. He said only this, *"You see that beautiful little girl? You see how she's laughing? You see how she's playing? If you want to see her grow up, you better never leave because I promise you, you will not have her. Something for you to think about."*

He then said nothing more; he stood up turned and went inside the house.

Chapter 8

A Weekend To Remember

I picked her up on Friday.

Elisabeth was so excited to tell me all the stories from the first few days of school. This was our time together. She had been with her dad for several days and it was time for us to get our giggle going and have a little fun. A pizza and a movie, treats, hugs and joys awaited us.

We pulled into the apartment building and she hopped out and said, *"Momma, I'll get the door for you."* I laughed. *"Well doll baby, you may need the key ya know? Here you go. Be careful of Rosie."* Rosie was her small grey tabby kitten who liked to meet us at the front door. I carried all the bags. Up the stairs she ran chasing Rosie with such glee.

"Oh Momma it feels so good to be home! Can we make those brownies now Momma? Can we? Can we?"

I laughed. *"Ok give me just half a minute or two to get things put away and then yes we can make the brownies. Why don't you go ahead and put your comfy clothes on and I'll work on things in here."*

"Okie Doke Momma Mosa," she giggled as she walked up the hallway to her bedroom. I put the groceries away and took out the supplies to make up the brownies. She came back in a pair of blue leggings and a striped top that had been one of her Christmas presents from the owners of God is good. There was so much joy and laughter together as we made the brownies and she got to lick the bowl.

"So what movie are we going to see today?" I asked.

"Secrets of the Mountain, of course."

"Well, of course," I replied and laughed. The adventurous heart of a seven year old knew a good

movie when she saw one and as with all her favorite movies she could recite the lines.

"You grab the drinks, I'll get the popcorn and the brownie," I told her. We curled up together on the big green sofa as she kissed my cheek and said, *"I love you Momma."*

"I love you too baby girl. Ok, are ya ready for an adventure under the mountain?" I asked.

"Oh yes!" she said with excitement and snuggled up in my arms and on my lap as we had the most wonderful evening together.

The next morning we went shopping. We found a beautiful white lace blouse and a sky blue skirt. We brought them home and I told her she could wear them to church Sunday morning. It was a large church a few blocks from our apartment. Elisabeth and I got connected quickly there. I sang in the choir and Elisabeth was involved in the Wednesday after school program where she loved to sing in the children's choir too. On the weekends when I sang on vocal team, Elisabeth would sometimes go with me. Knowing I was always a little nervous, she'd sit in the front row and would become my cheerleader.

"Sing loud Momma. I want to hear you," she would say and I'd smile.

"Thought I was supposed to say that to you?"

"Nope, I get to say that to you. I love you my momma."

"Love you too baby girl." Then, I'd go up on stage and Elisabeth would usually sing right along with us as we'd practice. I may have been preparing to help lead worship for a large crowd, but my heart really only had an audience of two – God and Elisabeth.

Elisabeth's heart loved God. So I tried to find little ways like a new outfit or a special treat as often as I could to help make church an extra special blessing for her.

After a wonderful morning shopping, we came home and Elisabeth played with her friends on the grassy area just outside our front door. She skipped up and down the sidewalk and twirled around like a ballerina. Her little cheeks were rose kissed from the level of activity and her hair wet from the humidity of the August heat. There were popsicles, water balloons, time in the pool, and a spur of the moment stuffed animal skit that held the beautiful sound of happy laughter. All this filled a most wonderful Saturday afternoon!

The evening held a bubble bath, games, stories, cuddles and pampering for my little adventurous *"princess of the most noble realm."* After prayers for the people she loved and a:

"Goodnight.

I love you.

See you in the morning.

Hope you have a good day tomorrow.

Nighty night.

Momma sure does love you."

Elisabeth drifted peacefully to sleep in my arms.

Sunday morning brought a rush of activity before church. Elisabeth wore the new little outfit we had purchased *"Oh, Momma, I feel so pretty today"* she said.

"You look beautiful sweetheart. Can Momma take a photo of you baby girl?" I asked her.

She giggled. *"Well, sure Momma."* Then she skipped to the living room wall and stood against it. Elisabeth was a natural ham and as she posed looking back at me with a side glance, her hands were clasped together and her bare feet showed in the spur of the moment photo. *"Ok, time to leave sweetheart. Go grab your shoes. Want me to pull your hair up real fast?"* I asked.

"Nope, it's good down Momma," she said.

Then, we hurried down the steps and out the door. As she climbed in the van I said, *"Look at that sky, baby girl. There's only one little cloud in it."* Then I asked, *"Tell me, what do you think that cloud looks like?"*

"Oh! I think it looks like a castle with a drawbridge Momma," she said as she climbed in her seat.

"Wow! You do? I just thought it looked like a fish."

She giggled at me and kissed my nose as I fastened her seatbelt and closed her door. I sat down, started the motor of the van and continued, *"Baby girl, did you know looking at clouds can fill your heart with dreams? God can take those dreams and make the most beautiful things. Promise me baby, you won't ever stop dreaming."*

"Ok. I promise. Momma does God always listen to our heart?

"Yes, baby girl. God always listens."

"So, that's just one more reason we should always talk to Him."

"Yes, just one more reason to pray."

"Ok. So Momma, I'll make you a deal, I won't stop dreaming if you'll promise me you won't ever stop praying."

"Ok. Baby girl, now that's a deal I can take! And, it makes your momma's heart smile too. I love you Elisabeth Grace Tobin, do you know that?"

"Yep, and I love you too Momma."

We pulled into the church parking lot as she finished singing the words *"Jesus loves me."* I took Elisabeth to her Sunday school classroom where the children's ministry pastor was her teacher for the morning and I went on to worship. Underneath the surface Elisabeth's heart was anxious. We both were. She told her pastor, *"My momma and daddy are getting a divorce."* He talked to her for a few moments, asked her how she felt about that and allowed her to share the emotion of her heart. He let me know that she had been concerned and I was grateful he had let her talk with him.

The church gave out *"Bible Bucks"* for attendance and Elisabeth was excited to receive them. The kids could redeem them for rewards or they could hold onto them for a Bible engraved with their name. Elisabeth had decided she wanted one of the Bibles and was looking forward to *"buying"* it when she had saved enough. After she said goodbye to her classmates and teacher we made our way out of the church.

As we left the service, Elisabeth was wearing a bracelet which said, *"Choose Life."* I noticed and asked her about it. With excitement she explained, *"We made this in Sunday School. It's to help us remember our lesson."* We talked more on the way home and Elisabeth told me, *"Momma, there are good things in life and there are bad things in life. We want to make wise decisions. If you choose to follow God His blessings become life, but if you don't choose God then things that happen are not good. So choose life Momma. Always choose life."* Nothing happens by chance. Divine appointments are everywhere around us. God understood hearing the words she spoke from the lesson would become enormously important for me.

After lunch Elisabeth and her friends decided to play with the hula hoop. We were becoming the apartment where the children gathered and my heart rejoiced. They were each taking turns. Elisabeth was cheering the others on, *"That's the way. You're good at that Brianna. No worries Casey. You'll get it. It just takes practice. It took me a long time to learn. Just keep practicing and you'll get it in no time"*

Then there was a little girl who came to play but she didn't own a hula hoop. Elisabeth stopped what she was doing, reached the hoop to the other little girl and said *"Here you go, God told me to let you have a turn with the hula hoop."* That evening she had come indoors and told her friends *"Goodnight, I will see you Tuesday."*

We spent the rest of the evening working, laughing as she dressed the kitten up in her doll clothes. We didn't have cable so we popped in a Barbie movie and worked on a cross stitch picture together.

Bedtime held a discussion regarding the hearing which would take place the next afternoon. She was anxious. *"What will happen in the hearing Momma?"* she asked.

"Mommy and Daddy will talk to a judge. Nothing for you to worry your pretty little head about," I told her.

"Momma, will Daddy be mad at me?"

"Oh honey!" l drew her close to me. *"Your daddy may be mad sweetheart, but no, he won't be mad at you baby girl. What we'll do tomorrow is important but if he's mad, I'll be the one he's mad at, doll baby. You don't have to worry about a thing. It will be just fine sweetheart."*

"God please let the court give me to my momma tomorrow. Please watch over my daddy. Would you bless us please, protect us and take care of the people I love, God?" These were the words of Sunday evening's prayer from the heart of a beautiful seven year old little girl.

Cradled in my arms, l stroked her cheek until she fell asleep.

Then l prayed, *"Please let the court give her to me. God, please watch over us, please. And whatever happens to me is ok, but God I don't want him to hurt her. Please."*

Monday morning came all too soon. l think the anxiety we both felt at that point was palpable. The sticky humid air of late summer was permeating the atmosphere with the feeling of the oppressiveness that this day would hold.

"Momma l wish l could just stay with you."

"I know sweetheart."

Gathering up all her belongings Elisabeth and l climbed into the red minivan and made our way toward her school. The blue sky was dotted with wispy clouds and the K-love Christian Radio station played softly in the background. There was a tense silence; no chat about *"What do you think you'll do today in class? Or ya know Momma, I'm gonna have a blast at recess today."* Our conversation was not that of the typical that morning.

As we approached the school the discussion began.

There was a long pause. l said, *"Baby, if everything works out you will be with me tomorrow. I want you to have fun today and not worry about anything. I'll call you later. We've already prayed and others are praying too. It's going to be ok."*

"Momma, will he hurt me?"

No child should ever have to ask that question. I said, *"No baby he won't hurt you."* I thought he'd hurt me if he hurt anyone, but a part of me was afraid too. We made it to school. She jumped out of the van, said *"I love you Momma,"* and closed the door. She walked toward the school then turned, smiled and waved and blew me a kiss.

This was the last time I saw my daughter alive.

Father, You are Jehovah – Checed, the Lord who is merciful.
I trust in you. Jehovah-Shalom, the Lord my peace.

Chapter 9

Countdown to Goodbye

I arrived at the court house first, shortly before 1:00 pm and took one of the many seats lining the right side of the wall in the austere hallway as I waited for my attorney to arrive. The interplay of the light casting shadows on the tile floor seemed to reflect the shadow of fear that gripped my heart as I worried about what this day would hold as I prayed for wisdom. *"Please God, please help us. Give me the words to say. Answer our prayers Father. Please."*

As a mom I wanted to protect Elisabeth. As a mom I wanted to deal with her fears. I knew my voice would be subjective. I knew there was no documented evidence of the things which were occurring. The only thing I could do was to try to give Elisabeth her own voice.

Elisabeth had seen a social worker just across the river. It was a larger city, but a different state. She was having nightmares of *"a woman standing outside a window getting her head cut off"* and experiencing things at her dad's which had me extremely concerned. He made her play a game called *"ghost girl"* and it made her very afraid. Elisabeth was six, almost seven, and cried often when I took her back to her father and her tiny little hands shook at times.

I didn't tell Jonathan that Elisabeth was seeing anyone because I was afraid of what could happen if he found out. The social worker documented her concerns of abuse in the home and made a recommendation Elisabeth spend as little time with her father as possible.

I spoke with the local domestic violence shelter several times about the best way to go about safely freeing Elisabeth and me from the situation we were in with Jonathan. They explained someone would be there with me when I went to court. I never requested a restraining order because even the domestic violence shelter representative was concerned that because Jonathan valued his weapons permit so much, it could potentially escalate matters if it was put in jeopardy. Sometimes things in life are better left unchallenged, and all I wanted was for Elisabeth and me to be safe.

The person at the domestic violence shelter had another appointment. She was not able to join me that day for court. I would have to do this alone. My family was back east. People I knew were praying, the church was praying, the people from God Is Good were praying but there was no one who had come to walk the journey of the afternoon with me except God.

Jonathan arrived. He said *"Hello Amy-o."* The name he used when he wanted to be playful.

I said *"Hello"* and turned away, nervous about what he may say. His attorney arrived. Deborah Adams was about five feet six. Her long dark hair was pulled up in a decorative hair clip and her navy and white scarf draped her gray suit. Deborah's strong confident demeanor easily showed that she was taking her job seriously. She spoke to Jonathan, and they stepped inside the chamber doors. A short time later he exited from the courtroom and took the first seat to the left of the door. I looked over and he raised his glasses with his left hand and rubbed his eyes.

What was he thinking? I wondered. What had she said to him?

Claire Thompson, my attorney, exited the elevator and made her way to me. She said, *"Hello, I'll be right back."* Her shoulder length red hair draped around her glasses. Her kindness instantly set me at ease. She walked the short distance through the hallway and stepped inside the courtroom doors.

When she emerged, Claire came back to where I was sitting. *"We're last. Because of the nature of this hearing she wants to get all the others completed first."* She explained. We would just wait until they called for us.

About 3:00 pm we were able to take our seat inside the court room. The warm wood paneled walls and neutral carpet did nothing to allay my anxiety as I looked around at the bench, witness stand, and desks for the attorneys. Behind the half size partition wall which separated the seats of the gallery from those cases actually being heard I sat growing more anxious as the minutes passed.

And I waited.

Finally, around 4:00 pm our hearing began.

I was called to the stand first. Claire made a motion for the court to accept the report and recommendation from the social worker Elisabeth had been seeing. The report documented the concern of abuse present in the home. She made the recommendation Elisabeth spend as little time with her father as possible.

Deborah objected on the grounds it had been completed in another state. She said there could be concern in the differences in credentialing state to state and there was no time to confirm or deny they were the same during the hearing. She also objected because Elisabeth's father was never notified Elisabeth was seeing anyone. The judge considered this for a moment and then said *"sustained."*

Claire looked at me. Deborah looked at Jonathan. He nodded to her and smiled. I knew without that report and recommendation giving Elisabeth a voice, no impartial witness to speak for her, no representative from the domestic violence shelter, the outcome of the hearing was in God's complete control.

Claire began her questions of me. *"Could you tell the court why you believe you should have custody of Elisabeth?"* she asked. *"I believe it's in Elisabeth's best interest,"* I said, and I explained as much as I could. Jonathan was using Elisabeth as a way to control me and I mentioned as much as I could so the court could adequately understand what Elisabeth was facing. Jonathan's attorney did a very good job in objecting to the things I was trying to share.

Deborah's job was to defend her client and she was trying. Still, that made it extremely difficult to share what I thought needed to be heard for the court to protect Elisabeth. The judge made notes on a yellow note pad as I spoke. Jonathan sat to the right of his attorney chewing gum and playing with the wrapper and within feet of the witness stand where I sat.

I explained on the surface the things that were affecting primarily Elisabeth. This hearing was about protecting her, not dragging her dad through the mud. I was concerned for my sweet Elisabeth. My hands began to shake as Jonathan would look up at me periodically.

Deborah asked, *"If you were so afraid of your husband why did you not request a restraining order?"* I started to respond to the question but she interrupted. *"Because the domestic violence shelter thought it would..."*

"Objection your honor – hearsay," Deborah retorted.

"Sustained," the judge said.

Deborah questioned me, *"If you were so concerned about the mental health of Elisabeth why did you never express that concern to her father?"*

"Because I was afraid for our safety once her father found out and I did not want to jeopardize either my life or the life of my child." I said.

Deborah looked at me and just shook her head.

I was grateful when she finally said, *"No further questions your honor."*

I stepped down and Jonathan was called to the stand. He had papers in his hand which he laid on the edge of the partition wall around the witness stand.

Deborah began questioning him. She asked Jonathan his response to the things I said.

He said, *"There was never any abuse inside our home."* Jonathan then began a discussion about me. To him, Elisabeth wasn't the heart of the issue, I was. He had been using Elisabeth to attempt to control me by propositioning me when he'd drop her off or I'd go to pick up Elisabeth saying that I could have more time to spend with her. *"There were three times when Amy and I..."*

The judge looked at me. My attorney looked at me. I looked at the judge and shook my head no. She thought for a moment and said, *"I'm not hearing that. This hearing is about a child and even if she did- if you were using sexual favors as a way for her to spend time with her daughter... I won't hear that in this court."*

Jonathan got upset. He said, *"Fine. If someone has to perjure themselves, fine."* He shoved the papers he had prepared to the side.

"Are there any further questions?" The judge asked Clair. She looked at me. Elisabeth had told me she was hiding in the closet to play. *"Ask him why Elisabeth is hiding in the closet,"* I whispered to Claire. She did.

Jonathan responded. *"I didn't know she was hiding in the closet."*

Elisabeth had said that her dad wasn't fixing her meals. *"Ask Jonathan why Elisabeth isn't eating at home. Why isn't he the one fixing her meals?"* I whispered to my counsel again. The attorney obliged.

Jonathan basically said that they ate with other people because it was more convenient.

No further questions. He stepped down from the witness stand and was seated by his attorney as the judge considered the case. I sat beside Claire, my hands clasped at my lips, praying the judge would think of Elisabeth. Praying she would protect my daughter. Hoping what I had said would be enough. *"Please God, please protect Elisabeth. Please God, please."* I prayed.

Those few moments felt like an eternity. *"I have made my decision."* The judge spoke.

I was so very afraid. Another whisper, *"Please God, please."*

"Custody of the child will be awarded to the mother. The father will be

granted visitation on Wednesday and Thursday evenings for 4 hours and every other weekend." She continued and addressed Jonathan directly, *"And when the child is with the father you are not to be going to someone else's to eat your meals. It is your responsibility to feed your child."* The gavel sounded. *"Court is adjourned."*

I whispered *"Thank you"* to God, to the judge, and to Claire. I got up and made my way to one of the meeting rooms just inside the courtroom doors to wait for my attorney.

Jonathan stayed behind. I heard him ask the judge, *"When will this begin?"* as I was walking toward the back. I turned momentarily to listen to her response.

"It begins immediately," was the answer by the judge. *"You all can work out the final details."*

I could hear him talking to Deborah but I could not make out anything else that was said.

My hands were shaking. My heart was pounding. I was choking back tears. Our prayers were answered! Elisabeth and I had prayed, so many people were praying and God had mercifully answered our prayers! All would be well. Elisabeth would safely be with me, and we would begin a life together in peace and in joy. Hallelujah! It was over. Elisabeth would be safe. Hallelujah! God answered our prayers. Hallelujah! All would now be well. The nightmare would be over!

Claire came, and we exited the courtroom. She sat down in a chair a short distance from the doors. I stood to the right facing her. Jonathan and Deborah exited the courtroom. I saw his face. A pang of fear. *"Please God,"* I whispered not knowing how he would respond.

He and Deborah stopped. There was discussion about when I'd pick up Elisabeth. It was already fast approaching 5:00 pm, and she had school the next day. By the time Elisabeth got dinner, retrieved anything she thought was important from her dad's home and got any homework done, got evening bath and bedtime routines done, it would be very late if I tried to press the issue to pick my baby girl up that evening; and how traumatic would it be on her if the transfer of custody happened if any of the emotion of the day was still present. Elisabeth was expecting to be with me on Tuesday anyway. So I decided it would be best for Elisabeth, and even for her dad, if I give them the evening together and picked her up on Tuesday, the next day. I was trying to be nice.

Jonathan then asked, *"So will she pay me now?"* Both attorneys said *"No."*

His attorney continued, *"You'll have to pay her child support."*

She turned to speak to my attorney. *"We'll get in touch together and work out the details."*

My attorney said that would be fine and Jonathan and his attorney exited the building.

My attorney turned to me, *"We'll give them a chance to get to their cars and then we'll leave."* I nodded.

"Amy you didn't raise your head the entire time he was near you," she said. I didn't say anything.

"You don't think he'll hurt her do you?" she asked as she thought for a moment.

"I don't think so." My heart was saying, *"I hope not."* I was becoming more and more apprehensive of what his response would be toward both of us and yet hoping and praying more and more that my worries were just unfounded anxiety. I was wrong.

"Ok, I believe we can go now," she said as she stood. We walked together and as we made our way out of the courthouse, gratefulness that God had heard and answered our prayers began to fill my heart.

ॐ

I was so excited to talk to Elisabeth. Since she was spending the night with her father I phoned her. Jonathan answered. *"Hello."*

"Hello. Can I speak with Elisabeth please?"

"Sure. Elisabeth, here, talk with your Mom. Take it in the other room." I could hear Jonathan tell her.

"Hi Momma," she said with joy.

"Hi baby girl. Did they tell you? Did they tell you that you get to live with me?"

"Yes, Momma I know! I can't wait to see you!"

Voices in the background...saying something to her.

"Oh ok. Momma, I have to go now."

She had been rushed off the phone.

"Ok baby girl. I will see you tomorrow. I love you sweetheart."

"I love you too Momma."

I made elated phone calls to my family, friends and people who had been praying for me. I was so relieved. God had seen us through. All would be well. A new life could begin.

A short time later I began getting text messages from Jonathan.

"When does this start?" he asked.

He was referring to visitation I figured. *"We can start this week if you want,"* I responded.

There was a short break.

"I'm going to look for a job in Newburgh," his text said.

"Newburgh?" I responded.

"I'll need to pick Elisabeth up from school," he replied.

"Elisabeth will be going to a new school," I said.

There were no texts for a few minutes.

Then he wrote, *"I will meet you at a place in between (his house and my apartment) tomorrow to give you Elisabeth."*

That was not the way it was supposed to be done. My petition for custody requested all transfer of custody meetings occur at a police station. *"What should I do?"* I wondered. *"Don't make him angry."* I thought. So I responded. *"Ok."*

I settled down and went to sleep. I was grateful that the Lord had heard and answered our prayers.

May our heart and lips declare your praise:
Jehovah – Magen, the Lord my shield
Jehovah – Rapha, the Lord my healer

Chapter 10

Night Falls

My world was about to crumble. My heart was about to shatter. Life would never again be the same. I woke up the next morning with the absolute sickest feeling I have ever had in my life and I knew that I should not meet him.

I sent him a text message that said, *"I'll meet you at the police station just tell me when."* That was at 6:00 am. He did not respond.

Nerves. *"Why isn't he answering me?"* I wondered. Still, no answer came.

At 6:30 am I looked at the clock and thought, *"Oh my God, he's mad at me!"*

"Should I call him?" I considered.

I was afraid now. I did not want to risk making him any angrier.

"What should I do?" I thought.

"No don't call him." I decided.

"He will have to say something later. Don't make him any angrier." I concluded.

At 6:30, he was killing my daughter

I went to work and waited anxiously for Jonathan to tell me when to pick up Elisabeth. But no word came. I just thought he was angry with me.

A policeman came to my office about 10:30 am.

"Are you Amy?" he asked.

"Yes," I said.

"You're not in trouble but you are going to need to come with us," he

said. *"Are those your supervisors?"*

I nodded.

"I need to talk to them a minute." He said. He stepped into the conference room and closed the door.

I heard a gasp and my heart knew. There was a woman, a social worker, who had come in with the police detective and I asked, *"Is my baby ok?"* She made a motion with her head to wait for the officer. He came out of the conference room and I don't remember the officer's words. The next thing I remember is being in the floor as the detective held my hand, the tightest it has ever been held, with tears in his eyes.

I can remember some details and not others. I can remember one detail at one moment and a different part on another occasion. I'm at peace with this aspect of the memories. I firmly believe this is the mercy of God tenderly protecting my wounded heart from remembering it all at once. That awful day and the next several which followed are both a welcome blur but also horribly seared into my memory.

I have since come to be able to associate a parallel mental image of Elisabeth smiling as she met our Savior with the events of that day. This softens the anguish of the memories. Still though, gratefully, I remember only pieces at a time.

At the police station, my pastor, Cory Fowler, knelt in front of me with tears in his eyes. He was on the Board of Directors where I worked and he was the Pastoral Director of Counseling for our congregation. He had baptized Elisabeth only weeks before and now he would preach her funeral. He told me Elisabeth had been shot five times. We later learned it was six.

Jonathan had sent out a final text message. It had not come to me. It was almost two hours later when it was seen. His final words were, *"Elisabeth and I are with Jesus...take care of Amy."* Then he executed Elisabeth, shooting her once in the back of the head as she lay sleeping in her bed. He still continued to fire, four more rounds across her tiny shoulder blade, one of which exited through her beautiful little cheek. Then, still one more gunshot to the lower part of her back. After that Jonathan shot and killed himself.

Everything seemed so silent for several days, as if I was removed from it and numb. The company I worked for had become, in many ways, an adopted family to me and they took me into their home. Lee and Gayle Williams had walked the entire journey since hiring me and now Gayle sat beside me on the sofa holding my hand, stroking it. I don't think she let it go.

The President of our Board, Dr. Christopher Albert, came and sat with me. He picked up the photograph that I held of Elisabeth. He held my hand and he cried with me.

I made a few calls to let people know what happened, but I remember only bits and pieces of the conversations. After making the final one, my heart emotionally turned off a light switch, and it did not come back on for two weeks.

I cried. It all felt surreal. I knew my heart was only touching the surface of the pain; I was going through a grief I couldn't feel the depth of yet. I remember being in the floor beside the bed crying and yet knowing in my heart that because the light switch of emotion had been turned off this was insulating and protecting me somehow from the depth of the cry my soul wanted to give. I cannot explain that, apart from God enveloping me in Him and knowing the limitations I could handle, He ensured it was not more than I could bear.

I had so many mixed emotions surrounding Jonathan's statement. He said that when he was about to kill my baby in cold blood. His own daughter. He had promised if I left I'd never have Elisabeth. He had hurt me time and time again, but he said *"...take care of Amy?"* What did he mean? Was this one final glimpse of love from the man I had dated and married? Was he instead directing someone to do the same to me? Did he truly believe that he could take life – the life of his own daughter and be rewarded with heaven? I was confused and my heart was so wounded.

Later, there would be threads God would allow my heart to see which would remind me of His love. However, in those beginning moments I needed the numbness to help cushion, and in a sense disassociate, from the overwhelming pain to my heart. This was exactly what God gave.

Elisabeth's lesson for that final Sunday was a verse from a passage of scripture found in the Old Testament book of Deuteronomy. God was speaking to His people, Israel, and providing clear direction about following His leading. It is a Chapter about the blessings of God when His people choose to serve Him and the curses we will experience if we choose not to follow His instruction

DEUTERONOMY 30:11-20

"Now what I am commanding you today is not too difficult for you or beyond your reach. It is not up in heaven, so that you have to ask, "Who will ascend into heaven to get it and proclaim it to us so we may obey it?" Nor is it beyond the sea, so that you have to ask, "Who will cross the sea to get it and proclaim it to us so we may obey it?" No, the word is very near you; it is in your mouth and in your heart so you may obey it."

"See, I set before you today life and prosperity, death and destruction. For I command you today to love the Lord your God, to walk in obedience to him, and to keep his commands, decrees and laws; then you will live and increase, and the Lord your God will bless you in the land you are entering to possess.

"But if your heart turns away and you are not obedient, and if you are drawn away to bow down to other gods and worship them, I declare to you this day that you will certainly be destroyed. You will not live long in

the land you are crossing the Jordan to enter and possess.

"This day I call the heavens and the earth as witnesses against you that I have set before you life and death, blessings and curses. Now choose life, so that you and your children may live and that you may love the Lord your God, listen to his voice, and hold fast to him. For the Lord is your life, and he will give you many years in the land he swore to give to your fathers, Abraham, Isaac and Jacob."

On the day of the funeral, the celebration of Elisabeth's life, I spent time with her alone. I wanted a closed casket to cushion the memories for my family from having to view the damage to her cheek. I needed to see her though, to say my goodbye to her.

Elisabeth was lying peacefully in the casket. Pastor Cory said, *"When you go in you'll see her. She has a scarf around her neck to cover the autopsy. You can lean over her but don't pick her up."* I wondered why, but I understood he must have a reason in telling me so I did not pick her up. Leaning over it, I tried my best to hug her.

She was dressed in the little white lace top and sky blue skirt she felt like such a princess in a few days earlier. I remember the softness of her face and touch of her hands in mine. I wanted so much to hold her, to pick her up and hold her. I wanted to rock my baby girl just one last time. This was my night. And the darkness that engulfed my soul was incredibly deep.

When the light switch of emotion turned back on, the grief was so overwhelming that it physically hurt to breathe. I had never experienced grief to that level. Every breath was so intensely difficult to take that my soul, not just simply my heart, felt as if it had been shattered.

God was there in those moments, but I could not sense His presence then. I had lost my child through her own father's hands. We were so close to being safe. So close to a nightmare all being over and done. Our prayers were answered but now instead, it was stolen, she was stolen. I had lost my beautiful answer to five years of prayer. My little Elisabeth Grace was gone. I had lost my trust in people and... my faith in God was shaken.

I wondered about her father's final thoughts. What things went through his mind? He had said he would not live without his gun rights and I've heard that documented abuse would have taken this from him. Is this what he was thinking? Did he think at all about Elisabeth?

He quit his job the night before this. Whatever he was thinking, the actions that Jonathan took in those final hours and moments were deliberate and intentional. The officers explained I likely somehow changed the outcome of Jonathan's plan when I told him I'd meet him at the police station. We just do not know fully in what way. We all suspect, I probably would have lost my life that day.

Elisabeth slept through it. That's a small comfort I have as a mother who misses her child every day. Because God prevented me from meeting him Elisabeth was able to peacefully sleep through the shots which took her life. At least she had not been terrorized, and she was not afraid.

The papers weren't settled from the hearing. It hadn't even been twenty four hours. Jonathan committed murder and had taken his life. Nothing had yet been signed and settled. In the eyes of the law, though a hearing occurred and the court had granted custody nothing was final. For that reason, legally I am considered a widow.

Within the month which followed, I settled details concerning Elisabeth and yet I finalized things regarding the person who took her life. I had to go before the court requesting items placed into my name to close certain files in connection with him. I was not remotely ready to act in that capacity for him, yet I had to do so.

Processing the emotions of losing a child at the hand of a parent is an especially difficult thing. There are phases to our grief and anger is one stage. I was grieving so very much – a love and marriage that had been lost, a child and answered prayer that had been ripped from my arms, a lifetime of memories and joy, my family, my trust in the God I served.

This was the hardest of the phases for me. Elisabeth's death was no accident; it was a clear and intentional act at the hand of a person who should have loved her. It was very selfish and cruel. In my heart, for several months I really did not know who I was angriest with, him for pulling the trigger, God for letting it happen or myself because I tried to protect Elisabeth and instead it got her killed.

People checked on me, but there was nothing they could do. I tried not to grieve openly. It was in private. There were a few who allowed me to be real with them then and still do. The darkness of this night was thick with heartache but still, God loved. His mercies were there even when I could not see them. In His love, He surrounded me with the people, the shelter, and the love which my heart needed.

The darkness was deep; still, God had planned long ago a path out of the valley and would gently teach me to faith again. In looking at myself though the mirror of His love, I could be real enough to be weak. I could be real enough to trust Him with what I was and where I was in those moments so He could teach me beautiful new facets of His goodness and His grace.

May you be lifted up in our life:
Jehovah – Jireh, the Lord my provider
Jehovah – Nissi, the Lord my banner

Chapter 11

Broken Mercies

Within the valley of the shattered heart, brokenness comes. The façade of strength gives way under the load of the burden and the weakness of humanity is revealed. What are the mercies which can be found in that? What is it a heart learns of God then?

In my heartache, this emotion of anger sometimes spilled over to others. I found myself taking it out on the people I loved the most. I needed an outlet for it somehow. The concept of placing the pain inside a *"pretty little box"* only worked in theory, for the attempts to contain the depth of heartache often worsened the brokenness within me.

This wounded shell I was on the outside was holding it together. On the inside, when no one was with me and I did not have to pretend to be strong, I was shattered, broken, and fearful. I had been betrayed in the absolute worst way by my own husband, the father of my child, the one person I should have been able to trust the most. If he had proven that I couldn't trust him, who could I trust? My life would become lessons in trusting again... both God and people.

For a time the *"what ifs"* of survivor's guilt plagued my heart in the silences of the lonely nights. What if I had just heeded Jonathan's warnings and stayed? Did he take Elisabeth's life simply out of anger with me? Would he have let Elisabeth live if he had killed me instead? Who would have died first, Elisabeth or me? Did Jonathan take his life at all out of despair for losing custody, just to hurt me or did he take his life over a gun? I will never know.

There will never be a moment when either killing another person or suicide is an acceptable way out of the challenges of life. We are never given the privilege of putting ourselves in the place of God. My husband's choices affected more people than only he and my daughter. With that one decision, the impact is now everlasting. Those who are left behind are permanently changed. Family will never see her grow. The people who were supposed to be touched and influenced by my daughter's life will never have that opportunity. The things she was supposed to do will never be completed, all because of the choices of another soul.

It is the love of God for His creation that allows us the opportunity to make our own choices. The free will He gives us which allows us the choice to serve Him in love, is also the same free will He gives us to make the decision to turn away. Even up to our very last moment, our very last breath God waits for us to choose Him.

Indeed, God knew the end of my daughter's days before she drew her first breath. Indeed, God saw how Elisabeth's life would end. God made provision through His promises to redeem the ashes of the wake created from the aftermath of her father's decisions. God taught me many lessons about how lives and legacies can carry on following our days here but He had many lessons to show me before I came to understand this.

In the depths of my most difficult valley, God wove His love for me. It took me time to see it, but it was there. It was entwined with His grace and it led me though the path that defined the dark season.

I busied myself during the day, doing the things I enjoyed and which made me laugh such as reading, sewing, getting lost on an adventure or taking a peaceful walk around a quiet lake. In the stillness of the night though, when it was just God and me, He alone knows the depth of the heartache I experienced in those moments. Even as a solid Christ follower who had walked with God for many years, who recognized the truth of the word of the living God, who had experienced His answered prayer in my life in beautiful ways, the depth of this valley was so incredibly difficult.

There were nights the pain in my heart seemed almost too great to bear. I missed Elisabeth terribly. I relived her death over and over in nightmares as I slept. It broke my heart. The hardest battles of the enemy are often fought in our weakest moments and the thought of simply going to sleep and never waking up crossed my mind on more than one occasion. Echoing in the stillness of those difficult and lonely hours would be the memory of Elisabeth saying, *"Choose life Momma. Always choose life."*

Yes, I was definitely choosing life. Even in the pain. When I was so wounded I could not love God, I loved people. It was only the determination I would not hurt the people I cared for which kept me from considering the passing notion of giving up, on a deeper level. To ponder its depths would have been to let my mind take me down a road I could not allow myself to go.

In the most basic way of understanding, I lived so others would not hurt like I was hurting. When I could not trust and could not pray, friends were praying and were listening to what God was placing on their heart. I would get a visit, a phone call, or a hug which lifted the heaviness again. They honored God without me saying a word and each made a difference in my life they may not have known they made.

God created every heart, every person for relationship. Connection has the power to both impact a person's life today as well as their eternal destiny. We each have a sphere of influence we can impact. From the brief and superficial interaction to sowing seeds of God's grace, to the depths of love, relationship is crucial.

I am asked often why I did not go home after this took place. There are several layers to the answer to that question. The main reason I stayed is that I believe I am supposed to be in the place where I live now. God is using the choice to stay to heal my heart, to strengthen me as a person and to teach me of Him in far greater ways than could have ever happened had I gone home. I left the town where I grew up full, with joy and a family. I would have returned there empty – with only memories. This would have eventually overwhelmed my heart.

The second reason is that over and over again Jonathan told me I would never make it on my own. I needed to show myself that with God I could make it in a place with no immediate family. Yes, God can use even a person's stubbornness to shape my heart and soul into what He wants me to become in Him. Here in a place I had no choice in coming to, God gave me the choice to stay. He gave me the choice to learn of His mercy, grace and love.

In those early days even the fact I buried my daughter here, kept me here. In staying, I gained strength, confidence, and God began to heal. When I was intensely lonely, I learned of a God who never leaves.

In my weakest moments God's love showed He cares. He knows the end from the beginning and God knew what I would face before it ever came to be a reality. Even Elisabeth's prayers of protection were both heard and answered – just in a way I did not and never will fully understand. God would not stop the free will of Elisabeth's father's choices, but He would be there to pick up the pieces that were created from it.

God would not stop the harm, but He would allow her to sleep through it. God Himself would protect her from ever being harmed again in allowing her to enter eternity. He would love her more than I ever could.

In taking me through such moments, God didn't deal harshly with my brokenness and the faith in Him which was shaken. Instead, He lovingly showed me that even in the worst moments possible, He was, is and always will be present. He continues to take each shattered piece of me and put it back together into something that is beautiful. Hopefully when others see me, they see God's mercy and a person much more beautiful because of the valley.

While healing may come instantly, much of the time healing is a journey. In just such a season as this, I was learning so many new facets of God, mercy, grace, forgiveness, love, and patience. The beauty of the beginnings of healing is a part of a valley as well.

In the brokenness of the darkness of my night, in this valley of heartache the Lord would shine much more clearly because I was weak. In what my heart saw as broken mercies, our Lord would do His finest work in my life.

God Is Good Foundation, my church, family and friends all played significant roles. When I could not pray, others would stand in the gap for me. He would take all those shattered pieces of the heart and restore it, with greater strength because of the weaknesses, for now the weaknesses drive the shattered heart deeper toward God. He shines much more gloriously through weaknesses in life.

It wasn't just by happenstance God allowed me to work in a Christian environment every day. Throughout this journey, God understood I would need to experience exactly the strength that comes as we surround ourselves with Christ followers every day.

I would not be where I am today in my relationship with Christ or in terms of my healing without that company or the people God had brought in my life for this season. It had been part of God's plan for me. In the people God surrounded me with He would continue to teach me of Him – a God who is always good, no matter what we experience in life. God understood for me to survive and journey beyond what I went through, I would truly need to know the truth of God's goodness.

I would answer the phone and talk about God's goodness with others when my heart did not feel it. I would say *"God is good"* when my heart was so broken and so angry with God that I did not want to serve Him. In just those words God took what was and reminded me that even in this valley He was still there.

God did not shy away from me honestly telling Him I was angry and I did not understand. How God could allow a child who prayed Psalm 91 (a protection psalm) every single night to not be protected? Why God did not keep His promise? Why He did not answer prayer?

PSALM 91

"Whoever dwells in the shelter of the Most High
    will rest in the shadow of the Almighty.
I will say of the Lord, "He is my refuge and my fortress,
    my God, in whom I trust."
Surely he will save you
    from the fowler's snare
    and from the deadly pestilence.
He will cover you with his feathers,
    and under his wings you will find refuge;
    his faithfulness will be your shield and rampart.
You will not fear the terror of night,
    nor the arrow that flies by day,
    nor the pestilence that stalks in the darkness,
    nor the plague that destroys at midday.
A thousand may fall at your side,
    ten thousand at your right hand,
    but it will not come near you.
You will only observe with your eyes
    and see the punishment of the wicked.
If you say, "The Lord is my refuge,"
    and you make the Most High your dwelling,
    no harm will overtake you,
    no disaster will come near your tent.
For he will command his angels concerning you
    to guard you in all your ways;
    they will lift you up in their hands,
    so that you will not strike your foot against a stone.
You will tread on the lion and the cobra;
    you will trample the great lion and the serpent.
"Because he loves me," says the Lord, "I will rescue him;
    I will protect him, for he acknowledges my name.

He will call on me, and I will answer him;
   I will be with him in trouble,
   I will deliver him and honor him.
With long life I will satisfy him
   and show him my salvation."

That Psalm was, and at moments is still especially difficult for me. This passage of scripture once gave both Elisabeth and me such peace and comfort. We would turn it into a prayer every night together. In the early days after her death I would cry out, *"Really God? Really? Where were you then? Where are you now?"*

I may never fully understand all the many whys. My heart faces fear and wonders if God knows I love Him, will He really protect me? I prayed and wondered will God really answer prayers for me? Will He really always be with me? Will He truly never leave? Will I really ever be safe? Can I trust Him? I once rested in His love, under the shadow of his wings. Can I rest there still?

For this passage of scripture, it is enough for me to say, *"God these words knot up my stomach and I don't understand, but I love you. I know you were there then, and you are here now. You understand my weaknesses, and I trust you. When it is hard for me to trust you help me to trust more."*

God has never asked me to toss aside the heartache of my past. He only asks me to trust within those broken mercies to the faithfulness of His love. In the beginning of the journey I could not pray at all, my faith was wounded so badly. Then, my prayers became simply tears before God. Now, I find that prayer time is taking on a lovely sweetness as I intercede for others.

It is still hard for me to pray for my own requests. My heart had learned faith. I held a miracle in my arms, I saw God do the impossible and it was ripped from me. I had prayed for protection, and yet, I had learned that the answer to my prayers is sometimes dependent on people being willing to accept God's will in their own life. He will not violate that person's will to answer prayer, even though the answer was provided. Sometimes because of a person's choices, the fullness of an answer to prayer may never come to pass.

Realistically, I recognize and trust that God is still healing the brokenness. God always hears prayer and He always answers. Yet, my heart still fears the human factor which can at times encapsulate God's answer.

My heart wants the big things of life: to be pleasing to God, to yield the throne of my heart to Him, to accept His will in all things. I also want the little things as well: new Chapters to life, to be happy, to feel loved, to be safe, to know in this big world I am never alone, to never be abandoned, to always pray and work things out, to not have to go to church alone, to spend time with someone who shares my life moments.

These are all God honoring requests. The next Chapter of my life is being written in God's plans for me. If it is God's will for my life now, it will be He who brings them into being and hold them together. Each one of those requests is still dependent on humanity yielding always to God. I have asked God to take my heart and do with it what He chooses. Life is about trusting, loving, growing and healing even in the hurts which can occur. My heart remembers a beautiful level of trust in God and misses it. It's coming, but I would still need to get through the transitions from the valley.

Chapter 12

Looking Glass Moments

The mirror of humanity always reflects the need for a Savior. In God's compassion and in my weakness, He would allow me to see my heart through the eyes of a Holy God to know the depth of my need for His grace. Those crimson threads of God were woven in my looking glass moments to draw me to Him.

The most significant turning point in the darkness of this valley occurred as I sat weeping on the worn beige carpeting of my living room floor. On that evening I had reached the depth of my grief. I argued with God, in excruciating heartache, in betrayal, in tears.

I was angry as I heard the sounds of children playing outside my window and my apartment was silent and lonely. I was angry with her father who was supposed to love and protect her. I took the bubble wrap which had been my stress reliever and on that night in my heartache I allowed it to portray the sound of the murderer's bones breaking as the bubble wrap popped when I twisted it. I threw a pillow across the room in my anger, picked it up and threw it across the room again. I was angry. Then I melted, weeping in the floor and cried, *"God you say you understand. But how can you possibly understand this?"*

God knew I needed him. He was the only one there with me and in His mercy He would begin to restore my heart. I picked up the Bible and God began to walk me through the death of His own Son. Because of all my sins, God's Son faced the death of crucifixion at Calvary. I sat weeping in the middle of the floor, tears streaming down my face reading the story of the death of Christ once again.

God did understand what I was feeling. His Son died too. Jesus died on a cross for sin. He willingly gave His life up, but the people who nailed him to that cross did so with every intention of taking His life.

God was so angry with humanity's sin and rebellion, with what was happening to His own Son and as our sins were placed on Jesus, God had to turn away. He could no longer watch the death of His Son. Even though I had given my life to God so many years before, the realization pierced my heart that it was my own sin with which He was angry. My sin had wounded God! It was not only my sin in general that Christ died for but it was that very evening, those moments, my actions and my feelings.

It was my sin for which His son died. God created the emotion of anger, and as this began to unfold in my heart and mind, I began to believe that yes, He understands it. He was angry just as I was angry. The sky became dark, and the earth shook violently because He was angry! He did understand how I felt, but He was not going to leave me there.

A beautiful process began that night of seeing the mirror of my sin through the eyes of a Holy God. In this deepest part of my valley, I had come to hate Elisabeth's father, murderer of my only child, my sweet Elisabeth Grace. My heart was so broken, no love remained for him then. God's word says *"Anyone who hates a brother or sister is a murderer, and you know that no murderer has eternal life residing in him."* (1 JOHN 3:15)

In that moment, I was no different than the rebellious murderer I hated. My sentence before a Holy God should have been the Hell I wanted for him. Yes, I cried out for God to forgive me but in doing so I also had to forgive the man who murdered my daughter. Obviously, that was not going to be easy.

While over time my heart would soften, I had to start quite simply. There was no point in trying to cover something that was not at all beautiful. I began in honesty with God, at just the place where my heart was in those moments. It was not a wonderful prayer. It was a prayer from the heart of a mother who had lost her child, at the hand of her own father, and a heart that was still angry.

How glad I am that God accepts us just where we are at the moment! How grateful I am that He chooses to never leave us at that point. In the looking glass moments this season of heartache and all it held, God's love remained.

I think in some measure the process of forgiveness will continue for me until I breathe my last breath. In forgiving, I am beginning to see the love of God in more profound ways, learning new lessons of grace I could have not known had this journey never occurred. On the days when it is harder to forgive, God lovingly shows me once more, a mirror of myself when I pray.

It is never done in a condemning way. Rather, God does it in a way that continues to strip away the things that need to be changed in my heart. It helps me to see that I stand in need of Him.

I need accountability in my life and I have been blessed with people who, in love, offer me this gift. It is something that challenges me to grow, keeps me pointed in the right direction and impacts my heart beyond words. God has placed wonderful souls around me who not only have walked the journey and come to know me, but who will also stand beside me, pray with me and when needed draw me back to God's throne.

In God's love for me He was beginning to redeem the brokenness through the work of forgiveness. He reminded me of two passages of His word; in the first one Samuel was talking to Saul after he had not honored God's instructions:

"But Samuel replied: "Does the LORD delight in burnt offerings and sacrifices as much as in obeying the LORD? To obey is better than sacrifice, and to heed is better than the fat of rams. For rebellion is like the sin of divination, and arrogance like the evil of idolatry. Because you have rejected the word of the LORD, he has rejected you as king." (1 SAMUEL 15:22-23)

And the second was a verse that Jesus spoke to his followers,
"For if you forgive other people when they sin against you, your heavenly Father will also forgive you. But if you do not forgive others their sins, your Father will not forgive your sins." (MATT 6:14-15).

I have been redeemed by God's grace, yet I am still human. As a child of the living Holy God, honestly choosing to look through the mirror into my heart, I sin. Daily I need the mercy of God's forgiveness. If I want God's forgiveness for my own sin, I need to forgive. That's a clear statement and a powerful thought!

This concept was echoed in a question from Dr. Albert as he sat down to talk with me one day. He asked, *"What if, in the time it took him to pull the trigger and the time it took him to breathe his last breath, Jonathan asked for forgiveness and was rewarded with heaven?"*

That simple question led into me having to consider the possibility which was before me. What if Jonathan did ask forgiveness and was rewarded with heaven but I refused to forgive him? What if I was eternally judged with hell for my own rebellion, hatred and unforgiveness as Jonathan enjoyed heaven with my baby girl?

That's deep, but God was beginning the work of mercy by showing me my true nature and my need for His forgiveness in my own life. It began as a choice for me. As I continue to see my need for God, this forgiveness becomes easier.

Over time as I prayed my heart softened. Saying *"I forgive him,"* was no longer just words. God reminded me He loved the world so much and it is not His will any should perish but that all should have eternal life (JN 3:16). This included Jonathan.

The first time I cried for my husband was profound in my heart. I cried in love for the man who I vowed to love, the man who took the life of the daughter for whom I had prayed. I cried and grieved at the possibility Jonathan would be separated from God, from Elisabeth, and he may endure torment for eternity. While it was also a bit surreal, I knew then true forgiveness was beginning to come.

I believe all life speaks now, both in our days on earth and our legacies which will follow us after we pass. So too, does Jonathan's life still speak. It speaks to the importance of love, loving God and loving others. It speaks to the importance of serving God from the heart, making wise choices and of never giving up in life.

Jonathan's life speaks to the importance of mercy, grace and forgiveness. It speaks to the compassion of God, and to the goodness of God even in the ashes of our lives. It speaks to the importance of never taking life for granted, always saying just one extra *"I love you"* to the people for whom we care the most. It speaks also to moving forward and living fully each day of this life we are given.

There are positive things I am seeing developing in my heart from this journey. Yes, I have weaknesses from that day, in being a little more fearful of people and having a harder time trusting. These weaknesses may in some measure always be a part of me now, but I have new strengths from the journey as well.

The strengths glisten as the precious jewels of God's love toward me. They are reflections of His healing and reminders of His grace. I love even more deeply now. A person's heart is even more important to me now. It is easier for me to recognize that even in the little things; we are impacting those around us every single day.

I also understand better the meaning of never giving up, no matter what happens in life. The weaknesses which have developed are no longer just simply vulnerabilities; they are things which keep me much more dependent on God. They let the transforming power of the Living God shine much more beautifully in life.

There are exquisite lessons of mercy which shine as diamonds carved by the Master's hand. As each new day unfolds, this new person I am grows stronger. I challenge myself to face head on the obstacles that are so large in my life.

Sometimes I fail, but I am trying to trust God a little bit deeper each day. In the vast supply of His mercies that are new every morning, I'm recognizing that He is God, always in all ways. Instead of my own will, my heart wants more often to say, *"Thy will be done sweet Savior."* I try to allow myself to no longer be controlled by the things or events of my past, but instead, allow God to always have His place of honor and see life continue moving forward.

I don't perfectly trust, simply believe, or wonderfully hope. But I try. In the daily little lessons, sometimes with faith as small as a grain of mustard seed the pieces of my shattered heart continue to heal.

The looking glass moments ask me to be fully honest with God, with myself and with others. Certainly, no one is really ever perfect or whole in this life. If we were, we would have no need for a Savior, so my journey is not yet complete. Because of the depth of the betrayal and shattered trust, the healing coming through the threads of God's love is creating a new heart. Sustained vulnerability with both God and others is bringing such a rich depth of healing to my heart. It became the steps out of the valley and in sharing the truth of my *"weaknesses,"* God brought strength and a beautiful new life in Him.

PART THREE

May the fullness of God's love
and His mercy
shine as treasures
to be found in every horizon.

Chapter 13

Same Story: New View

"Amy, how did your perspectives change?" was the question from the elderly individual Elisabeth left flowers for in our apartment complex. Thin and frail, Mrs. Jenkins didn't often have many visitors. Her children all lived far away. I took her dinner and spent some time with her. Without fail she would weave wonderful thoughts into our time together. Her prayers blessed my heart and the wisdom of her questions would invite me to go deeper with God.

She continued, *"Amy, you've encountered many things since losing Elisabeth. Beyond just missing her, how your life is different now?"* Interesting question I thought.

"God never allows anything that isn't meant to change us." She said.

"Well, yes that's true. Hmmm, let's see...." I began.

Shattered pieces of a heart do not heal overnight. There is always a period of transition. No matter how deep the valley is, the journey through it is a transition between the past and the future. The heart changes as one accepts the past as that which breaths beauty into the present and knowing that through God, it also provides the fertile soil of the tomorrows ahead.

"My past isn't exactly a light topic." I told her.

Questions of introduction used to be so simple. *"Tell me about yourself." "Do you have children?" "Tell me about your family." "Where are you from and how did you end up here?"* With my past though, they are not really that simple any longer.

Navigating the responses of others has been a challenging transition. Realistically, it wasn't just my family which changed. Daily life changed. Not only for me, but also for the people who know me or learn my story. There are times I worry about opening myself up to new people. If I work on building a relationship, and I'm open with my past I have to take them through some treacherous waters so to speak and I risk people walking away or not knowing how to respond.

I'm also not really the easiest person for my friends to introduce. Imagine how you'd go about something like that. *"I have a friend named Amy. I want you to meet her but there are things you need to know about her first."*

To some who hear my story, it provides hope for his or her own struggles. Almost as if by me choosing to share it and move forward beyond it, this gives them permission to feel and heal from their own while hopefully, recognizing God's love in the midst of their journey.

To some, my past is an area where people may get stuck. Some feel it's a deterrent from involvement. *"She's been through too much."* They may discount or miss the blessing of what my life, experience, prayers, love brings to the table. For others, protection goes to making decisions for me, *"I don't think she's ready."* Instead of extending the same freedom to me they wish in their own life – to be, to do things, to try, fail and try again. My valley was so deep in their own mind, that any emotion I do show or any lack of trust isn't just the heart of a new person with a past, but instead a sign that my healing is still not complete.

To some, I'm an incredible inspiration who displays great strength and forgiveness *"Amy, you are so strong,"* is a statement I've heard many times. Yet, it never has been my strength that people have been seeing. No one is strong through something like that. Instead, it has always been the power of the God who is faithful to His word. I was not strong because of some characteristic I had. No, I lived in an atmosphere of significant struggle for more than a decade. What people saw was the promise of God lived out in my life as He promised in ISAIAH 41:10:

"So do not fear, for I am with you; do not be dismayed, for I am your God. I will strengthen you and help you; I will uphold you with my righ-

teous right hand."

To me, the valley was never meant to define me or determine the outcome of my life. I was not meant to be known simply as the *"mother of the child who was murdered by her father."* God takes all that my past has been and because of the past, He will shape the present and unveil the future. Deep in my soul there is a part of me that the enemy did not touch. God is bringing that part to the surface. All wounds heal, it's the scars that will teach us and transform us through the mercy of God.

"I see," she said. The evening sun was now showing on her face. She was squinting somewhat and I got up to lower the blind. *"Thank you Amy."*

She proceeded, *"Yes, I can see both sides of that. I suppose everyone has had to learn to adapt. It can be a lot for people to take in, but you're learning to balance it well from what I see. And yes, you are also on the edge of your future my dear."*

"I think Mrs. Jenkins I'm probably too close to see all the changes in me. My little sister, though, probably best summed up what she has seen develop in one of my conversations with her. It makes me grateful for what God is doing in my heart, especially if other people can see it."

Vanessa had explained to me, "The changes I see in you are both strengths and weaknesses. You are more at peace than you have been since you met him (Jonathan). You are more confident in who you are, instead of who people say you are.

"You understand you are worth something again. You see the value in people getting to know you again. You know your limits better and you no longer do things simply to please someone else.

"You are not overly trusting any longer and you recognize more fully that people make their own decisions instead of accepting the responsibility on yourself. Where once you would have said 'I made him hit me' you recognize that you are not responsible for the choices people make, good or bad.

"But I also see that you don't trust enough sometimes, you do still struggle with a little survivor's guilt at times and you don't push yourself beyond your comfort zone very easily any longer."

Mrs. Jenkins rocked back and forth for a few moments with a smile on her face. *"Yes, I would say those are some pretty big changes Amy."* She said, as I went to get her another glass of sweet tea and a piece of apple pie for dessert. I sat back down on the ivory sofa just beside her mauve rocking chair and placed the pillow to my side.

"Dear, I'm enjoying your company this evening," she said. *"I would like to see things through your eyes Amy. Would you share with me what new things you're seeing in God's word because of this journey?"*

I smiled at her, understanding she was trying to get me to stay a little longer. *"Ok. Well, I guess a few things have kind of changed...."* I began.

The stories I once read took on fresh new meaning. No longer were they simply inspirational thought or a principle for my heart, but the scriptures reflected beautiful nuances and the intricacies of individual lives with all the thoughts, emotions, strengths and weaknesses as we have in life still today.

I looked at the heart of Joseph in a new way. Oh what heartache it must have held for him as his brothers threw him into a pit then sold him into slavery. What cries must have come from a heart that thought he would never see his father, his brother Benjamin or his family again!

More than 2,000 years later, in the silence of an empty apartment and with a blanket of snow falling outside my window that mirrored the shattered pieces of my heart gently falling into the blanket of the love of God as I knelt, I was overwhelmed picturing Joseph's tear stained cheeks caked with mud from the dust of the pit. Can you hear the anguish of his heart as the young boy would have begged his brothers, *"Please, please don't do this!"* How many times I had begged *"Please, please don't do this"* when my husband was angry as his hardened heart used weapons of words or hands to wound me. Although the situations were different, the parallel left the traces of tears on my cheeks as I wept for him.

As his story progresses, Joseph is raised up into the purpose of his life. He would never have become the person he was without experiencing the challenges in life he faced. I was coming to accept that even through the most painful experiences, God is still God, and nothing touches our life without God allowing it.

Joseph said to his brothers from a heart of deep faith, words of wisdom forged from a relationship with the God who had never left his side: *"You intended to harm me, but God intended it for good to accomplish what is now being done, the saving of many lives."* (GENESIS 50:20). Those words struck my heart in such beauty and magnitude. Yes, if it was real in Joseph's life and God is no respecter of persons, so too, it will be real in my own life somehow.

"And..." she continued with a grin. *"What? All that wasn't enough for her? She still wants more?"* I thought as I smiled at her. She challenged me to consider things. Have I said how much I like that lady?

"Well of course, there's Job...." I told her.

I read the passage that described how Satan came to God. He requested God release the hedge of protection around Job's life. Not only did this enemy have to ask permission to do anything, a loving, compassionate, merciful, caring God had to grant that permission.

That's a massive thought!

My heart no longer could even minutely relate to *"name it and claim it"* gospels. While we may long to believe that if we serve God all will be well and nothing bad will ever happen, it's just not the case. I had lived it. I served God, God had answered my prayers and I held a miracle but I still had that gift stolen from my life.

Jesus reminds me in John 10:10 *"The thief comes only to steal and kill and destroy..."* Job lived that as well. God allowed this all because He understood the end from the very beginning and even in all that occurred, God loved? Yes, indeed. Why? Because of the last part of John 10:10 ...*"I have come that they may have life, and have it to the full."* There is an enemy we all face and there are struggles we all may endure but our trials will surely fade away and there is a Savior who has defeated the enemy forevermore!

Even in difficulty and challenges my life had been so blessed that I had once glossed over the scriptures that told Job's story and wondered about the weakness of his faith. I also had once wondered how Job's wife could respond the way she did.

"His wife said to him, "Are you still maintaining your integrity? Curse God and die!" (JOB 2:9).

It took my valley to begin to understand the immense depth that Job's story holds of God's love, His mercy, our humanity and how God redeems faith.

As I read and reread the story in my valley, I could see my own reactions in those of both Job and his wife. They lost absolutely everything. For a while Job's wife was angry and Job was depressed and insolent. A mother lost not simply one child, but all then and all at once.

From one broken heart to another I was able to now see the tremendous ache of desperately wounded hearts in a conversation between them.

"His wife said to him, "Are you still maintaining your integrity? Curse God and die!" He replied, *"You are talking like a foolish woman. Shall we accept good from God, and not trouble?"* (JOB 2:9-10 NIV)

God was redeeming my faith through their story. We don't always cause our own valleys. Job had no choice in his valley and his valley affected both him and every member of his family. God had to reveal Himself to Job because he was human. God, however, did not draw Job back in until he was ready to hear what God had to say to him. In the end, *"The Lord blessed the latter part of Job's life more than the former part"* (JOB 42:12) but it took time to journey through the valley.

"And so, if the people of the Bible are becoming more real to you Amy, tell me about Jesus," she said with a smile. I laughed a little.

"Ahhh, is that where you've been heading all along, Mrs. Jenkins?" I asked and she grinned as she finished her meal. *"You're sneaky,"* I teased *"But ok let's see...."*

We are never told how the events that Joseph or Job experienced changed them. I can imagine they were changed, even as God was changing me. I began to wonder what weakness were seen because of their experiences that held them even more closely to God's side, what gifts of strength were within their character that specifically equipped them to journey through their difficulty to the other side of faith? How did their relationship with God deepen because of it?

Even Jesus has become more human to my heart. The story of Matthew 26:36-46 came to life for me. In your mind's eye, see our Savior with his olive skin talking with His disciples, His feet and sandals dusty from each step as he walked, tassels tied to the four corners of his clothes to remind him of the commands God had given to His people. See the pensive expression on his face as his mind drifts to that which lay ahead of him. See his beard and hair moist with the perspiration of a heart in agony. See Jesus enter into the Garden of Gethsemane surrounded by the gnarled wood of the olive trees. *"Stay here and keep watch with me,"* He tells them.

Asking Peter, James and John to go with him, Jesus walks on a little further, every beat of His heart increasing the deep heaviness and overwhelming heartache he felt. What is the reason our Savior would ask them to come? Hear the emotion in His voice as he tells them, *"Wait here. Keep watch. My soul is deeply grieved,"* and see him go on a little further and then fall on his knees and then to his face in prayer. Do you hear the agony of his heart as he cries out, *"My father, if it's possible let this cup pass from me"?* Can you hear the acceptance as he says, *"Yet not my will but thine be done"?* Did you recognize the Savior spoke to His creation and pleaded *"Stay with me...."?*

There is so much depth in those words for me now. This concept of God I once accepted with my head and my heart superficially, but it was not until my valley that I began to accept Him in His humanity and to begin to see HIM. That changed absolutely everything!

God reveals in such sweetness precisely how He has chosen the places and the people who can influence us the most during the seasons of life. From each category of individuals, God reminds us somehow that the spheres of impact we have on each other are great. Family touches our heart in their own unique way, as does church, friends and others. These are the ones who God places as beautiful jewels of His mercy for our heart.

Family can be there and with a genuineness which defines family alone. Church can point to the throne of God and friends can sometimes be there when no others can be with us. It was not His family who Jesus took to Gethsemane. It was not the people from His temple who knew Him. It was the people who were with Him in that moment.

Who are your three? I have lived my Garden of Gethsemane, my valley of the incomprehensible, the darkness that engulfs the soul. How important it is to walk in mercy and love with those who walk this journey of life with us.

Our visit ended with wonderful smiles, prayer together and a hug. *"Mrs. Jenkins, do you know how much you bless my heart?"* I asked her as

I gathered my things and got ready to leave for the evening. *"Oh probably about as much as you bless mine."* She said with a smile. She had asked me to put into words the new perspectives of the Bible and of Christ himself that I had learned from my valley. I had made the visit to make her smile, minister and pray with her but in the end, it was she who had done that for me. May your mercy and grace fill our life,

Jehovah – Tsidkenu:
the Lord our righteousness.

Chapter 14

Ripple Effect

A soft smooth pebble or a rough jagged stone creates the same type of ripple across the surface of a still, peaceful lake as it is dropped into the water. So too, l am beginning to see beautiful ripples of God's redemption radiating softly outward to replace His mercies for the heartache once known. It is said in Isaiah 61:3, that God,

"provides for those who grieve in Zion—
to bestow on them a crown of beauty
instead of ashes,
the oil of joy
instead of mourning,
and a garment of praise
instead of a spirit of despair.
They will be called oaks of righteousness,
a planting of the Lord
for the display of his splendor."

The crimson thread of God's love that weaves its way throughout the story of His mercy in our life stands out against the backdrop of the darkness which invades any valley. The strands of God's grace and goodness allow the pattern of redemption to be woven offering hope for a heart to believe that God's love always remains. It flows beyond the pain and beyond the valley to the future in Him still yet to be. The ripples of redemption will still continue to flow.

The questions now are not so much about the details of the loss. Instead, they are about how my heart is growing. They are questions about how my faith is remaining and what l want my tomorrows to become because of the journey.

The stone that fell into the waters of my life had been meant by the enemy to destroy my heart and my faith. Yet instead, it has become the impetus for the beautiful transitions created as I begin to recognize more deeply the mercies of God's love.

In the valley those I met asked specific questions about what had taken place, but time and time again the questions came from those who had been wounded and their questions longed for peace in their own pain. Through tear filled eyes their questions would search for answers.

"Tell me, how did you come to terms with that?"

"Tell me, how do you forgive the unforgivable?"

"Tell me, how do you find the faith to go on?"

"Tell me, is there really hope?"

Oh yes, precious one, there is hope! The faith to go on comes from the God who gave us the faith to believe from the beginning. He sustains His people. How do I forgive the unforgivable? Because, I am a sinner who has been forgiven much. How do I come to terms with my past? By recognizing that it is just that, my past. By recognizing that there is a *"today"* to be lived and a *"tomorrow"* to hope for.

What a beautiful picture of God's grace to take the unimaginable story of one soul and allow it to open the door for healing in another!

I have received invitations to share with churches what God has been doing in my life. The requests came from individuals and Pastors who recognized that within their church were people whose hearts were breaking. They understood I hold no formal training in addressing congregations with the message of Christ, only that I had a heart and a testimony they believed God may somehow use to reach one who needed His touch.

In honoring their requests to share, I went. Time and time again I would see hearts that ached to find God's hope. The questions I mentioned find their way into the after service discussions that take place with me. They are the same in every church, every meeting.

As I share, God ministers to me as well. In telling my story, I am allowing God to reopen wounds in my heart and pour out my soul to many I have never met. I also need God's healing to continue to touch my soul shaping the deep recesses in me into more of a reflection of Him. Sharing the story openly continues to help to bring freedom to my heart and countless others. In doing so often the feelings of shame or heartache for the painful things we have experienced are lifted and God is glorified through them. In both the good and difficult aspects of honoring God's leading, the messages last far beyond the thirty minutes of so in sharing a testimony with others.

I was called to a church in rural Ohio, just across the river from the town where I was raised. On a cold January morning five months to the day from the court hearing, God redeemed ashes. He turned them into a beautiful moment that glorified Him and took His healing to a greater level not only for me but also for one particular family.

To my left, as I stood in the pulpit were two women. I had never met them. They came specifically to hear a story quite similar to their own. There were many who were moved to tears as I shared what God had placed on my heart and as I looked around the room I saw their tears as well.

With the valley so fresh, the very fact that God had chosen to flow through Elisabeth's story touched me. Following the service we were able to spend a few moments together discussing our experiences. They had lost not only one child, but two also through a murder-suicide at the hand of a parent. We encouraged one another in ways only those who have encountered a related valley can understand.

I shared with the congregation of another church and after the service a gentleman with tears streaming down his face came to tell me he was dealing with the loss of a family member. The ache which remained in his heart was so very great. He shared how hearing a simple story of a valley of weeping had reminded him that there was hope in his own. God could bring peace.

It didn't take long to see the story of God's mercy through this journey was greater than me and it reached far beyond the scope of my little circle of acquaintance. I was simply the steward of opening the *"pretty little box of emotion"* many hide the pain inside to invite God's healing to begin or continue to flow. Through letting me live, God allowed me the opportunity simply be a vessel to encourage the progression of deeper relationship with Christ and new testimonies of faith in many people as he redeems that which was meant to destroy.

God's ripples of redemption flowed into the life of a young woman, who was passing through the community on business and was moved enough by a story she heard in a news release to contact my pastor to meet me. Over lunch we spent a few moments talking about God. We sat at the table for more than an hour as she told me her story, and then asked mine. *"Amy you don't realize just how much I appreciate you sitting down with me. You are a testimony of God's grace and you have made a difference in my life. Please understand that though I live in another state I have been praying for you and my church has been praying for you. The fact that you chose to sit down with me, a total stranger, and be so open with me makes me believe that in my situation there is always hope."*

Time after time, within each person who shared his or her own stories with me, was a heart that longed to hear the whispers of hope for their circumstances. A heart that longed to, just for a few moments, lay down the façade of strength, and to open their heart to the healing of God's love. People who wanted to receive release from the pain they were trying to hold both beautifully and deceptively wrapped in their own *"pretty little box."* It is always an amazing thing to behold.

೨

Sometimes I stand in awe of God as He seemed to orchestrate unplanned moments to reach the heart of a hurting soul. God has been allowing the ripples to influence children. What glorious ripples God would design in His mercy to reach the lives of children so that I could see Him bless them! In this, God is working to continue to heal that part of my wounded heart, to release its pain, to beautifully move beyond the valley toward whatever future horizons of joy He yet holds in store for my life.

Every life has a purpose. The longest life has many stories to tell of the opportunities to witness God's hand. The shortest life holds the eternal treasure of impacting lives as a testimony of God's creation because of a precious heartbeat. Elisabeth's life was no different. She had a wonderful purpose in so many beautiful ways.

An inner city church had given me an opportunity to be involved in their Vacation Bible School program. I taught a Bible story through a drama skit and following the lesson would join the kids in their mission project in the basement where they filled shoe boxes for Operation Christmas Child. As I was filling my box, I met a child who was in Elisabeth's class at school and was a friend of hers. I had never met her. I was told how profoundly Elisabeth's passing had affected this sweet little girl and how this child would cry and cry for Elisabeth.

She was standing on the far side of the room placing stickers in a shoe box. Her blonde hair was pulled back from her face in a pretty lace barrette. I made my way toward her. *"Emma, this is Elisabeth's mom,"* the woman who had brought her to the Vacation Bible School explained. Emma began to cry. I knelt down on my knees and gave her a hug. Brushing a tear from her cheek I looked into her beautiful blue eyes that were so sad in that moment and I choked back my tears too.

I said, *"Emma, thank you for being Elisabeth's friend. It's my pleasure to get to meet you. She cherished each friend she made and that makes you very special to me,"* I told her. We shared a few stories about Elisabeth and talked about the tree that the school had planted in Elisabeth's memory. I said, *"Please don't feel sad about Elisabeth. She's in heaven now and will be forever safe. We'll get to see her again one day if Jesus lives in our heart and oh, can you imagine all the stories we'll share?"* We talked about her funny personality and Emma smiled once more. Then I stepped out in the hallway and choked back tears. Not only did I have to deal with missing Elisabeth, but one selfish action had wounded and traumatized so many people. I left a little early that day, stopped at the cemetery and just cried.

That same inner city church gave a children's program I was a part of the ability to use its fellowship hall each week. The local Rescue Mission catered meals for the at risk youth we served. We had two children in the program tell us the meal we served was the only meal they had eaten all day.

Another child involved in the program was named David. He was six years old. On the first night he joined our program he sat in the floor and colored. We tried to engage him and asked *"Would you like to play a game or sing a song called Jesus loves me"?* He looked at us with his sand brown hair parted to one side and big blue eyes and said, *"Who's Jesus?"*

The adults were a little surprised. We probed a little more and found out he not only had never heard of Jesus, but he had never set foot inside a church. We obviously arranged for a tour. He became the most faithful child in the program and its biggest cheerleader, inviting several others to join as well.

At the close of each Monday evening session we would circle up together. Joining hands I'd ask, *"Ok. What are we praying for this week? Who wants to start?"* They would go around the circle and each one would share a prayer request with the others.

Then I'd say, *"Who wants to pray?"*

Every week they took turns but David prayed most often. Not one of the kids in our group had a Bible. A family purchased brand new Bibles for each child and presented them as gifts. David liked his

Bible so much he slept with it under his pillow. In the end we saw all the kids involved in local churches. As for David, not only did he begin attending church, but his entire family did as well. Before drawing that program to a beautiful close, there were fourteen children who prayed Jesus would come into their heart and there were entire families in church simply because God redeemed the ashes of one child making the journey to heaven.

God answered prayer and shared with me the life of a beautiful and precious little girl. My heart was eternally changed, my family was transformed, and Elisabeth's friends were influenced by all that made her special and unique as a child of the Living God. The Lord has still continued to allow Elisabeth's life to influence many people she never met and in ways I never could have dreamed.

As Elisabeth's mother, my heart will always miss my little girl. I would rather she be here with me or I be with her. That's a mother's heart. Still, God creates beauty out of ashes. I'm watching God be God in miraculous ways to transform life here, near and far away today and for generations to come.

Because Elisabeth went to heaven, the God Is Good Foundation graciously funded the building of an orphanage dormitory in Myanmar that houses twenty little girls. We chose the project and the location for a purpose. This place was chosen because it has one of the highest rates of human trafficking. A dormitory was chosen because it makes a difference for many years to come. Grace House, as it is named, declares to all who would live there that God is good no matter the circumstances of life.

These same precious children once at risk of being sold into slavery now have a safe place to lay their head and call home. They are being nourished and fed in the shelter of that building. They are also receiving an education and hearing the gospel of Jesus Christ. Because hearts honored God and went the extra mile to give, these girls will now have the beautiful opportunity to impact the world around them as our next generation of social impact leaders.

After these children leave the orphanage to begin a life on their own and they have children, the building will still remain to shelter new children who need the same love, care and mercy these first group of girls needed. In this way, the ripples of redemption flow ever outward continuing into an ever widening circle of God's mercy and His love.

None of these things would have ever been birthed into existence had there never been a miracle of answered prayer, or the life of a beautiful precious child. No, it was not God's plan that ordained the death of a child. No, a free will would not be violated to save her life. Yet, God would transform the action which stole that miracle into something that for generations shall stand as a testimony to how the ripples of redemption of God's love continue always to flow outward.

There is yet one other beautiful way God's hand can be traced. In the hopelessness that could sometimes define a prison system, God has taken the story of what happened to a beautiful little girl and how no matter what our lives hold, God is good and He has touched the hearts of those in two prisons in Ohio.

The incarcerated men and women are themselves telling this account of how that same crimson thread of God's love can be seen no matter the valley of life we experience. It is not the story of the valley and the journey is not the part that is the most telling; it's the hope that people are finding in the middle of their own darkness because God's love is faithful.

The hand of God creates beauty from ashes and just as Joseph declared so I can now say *"You intended to harm me, but God intended it for good to accomplish what is now being done, the saving of many lives."* (GENESIS 50:20).

Yes, a glorious serenity fills my heart. The faithful love of God will forever stand. Now that is a beautiful perspective of peace.

May you lead us, strong, protecting One
Jehovah – Rohi, the Lord my Shepherd
Jehovah – Shaddai, the Lord is mighty

Chapter 15

Anticipating Beauty

There is magnificent beauty all around us that declares the splendor of God. The valleys of life come gloriously to an end in the new beginnings of such radiant hope. Taking the glistening treasures of lessons learned in the valley into the newness that defines the pathway ahead, creates an atmosphere of expectancy as the route winds ever forward in our relationship with God.

The valley fades in its immensity to become a tool of shaping in the hand of a skillful master. It allows God to stand gloriously as the Lord of the valley as much as He is the Lord of the blessing. Anticipation grants hope and purpose to any heart which has been wandering through the night seasons of a dark and complex valley.

I had once been reminded to choose life and exist. As the grip of the valley's hold continues to weaken and diminish through the healing mercies of a wonderful God, the threads of His love beckon me to choose life and live once more. I choose to receive all that life is and move beyond merely surviving to step into the pleasures that life holds, once more to accept the beauty of life in the vibrancy of serving a God who makes all things new.

I choose to accept where I am at this moment. The weaknesses leave me open to the blessings of future lessons, more dependent on the strength of God's mercy. Receiving the beauty of the work He will continue to do in my heart, I choose also to accept the strengths that have come and the newness of life in Christ.

I choose life with all the fullness, the pleasures, the promises of

God's love. I move beyond the valley, never to be defined by its weaknesses but propelled by its blessings. I choose to allow God to take that which is and shape it into that which it will become as I look to a living God and anticipate beauty in the moments of today and the mercies of tomorrow.

The journey has helped me understand that each day there are two paths which can be taken, multiple times throughout the day, and it is my decision which one I will select. I had a decision to make on the day the valley began. So did Jonathan. We were making life and death decisions in the most distinct ways. Would I listen to my will and go pick up my child as had been planned out by Jonathan, or would I listen to the overwhelming impression in my heart that I shouldn't meet him any other place but the police station?

Jonathan made a decision to follow his own will through a life and death decision which affected not only him but his own child and all who were touched because of her. On that day, the protection of God was my life and death decision. Had I chosen my own will the outcome of the events of the day would likely have been very different. I had to choose God's will even though I did not know the valley which lay before me.

I still have those same two paths to choose in my heart throughout each day. The first trail becomes the path of my will. This may look pleasant to the eye and be a wonderful road paved with many nice things which could distract us from the depth of God's mercies and grace. It is a pathway where I set myself up to be my own God and my free will becomes that to which I surrender.

Then, there is the second pathway; it is the path of God's will. It may seem simpler. It may seem as if the blessings are not as obvious or the path could appear much more difficult to travel. The path of my will leads me away from my God, but the pathway of God's will leads me toward Him.

May God always order all of our steps to choose the correct path and always choose His will. If our feet stumble, may He always pick us up again, helping us to choose Him, always. Simple choices, decisions of pathways, define the destiny our life will take as we yield our moments forever to the God who knows the end from the beginning.

I sat on an empty beach one crisp Thanksgiving morning wrapped in a blanket. The cool breeze, the fragrance of the salty air and the sound of the ocean waves made me grateful for the moment. A friend had taken me to Jacksonville Beach, Florida, to spend the holiday. Misty allowed me to come and go as I pleased, aware I was still processing the emptiness of holidays without Elisabeth.

On that morning, I sat for hours watching the darkness of night be vanquished in the soft light of the morning sun as it rose over the horizon of a vast ocean. How perfectly it alluded to that which was taking place in my life. All was well with my soul once more. The sound of the sea coming into shore reflected the power of the God who had been with me in the deep of my life.

Had I been alone on a beach in the middle of the valley, the result likely would not have been the same. With the darkness of the valley behind me and the horizon of joys that still lay ahead, there was such significant beauty sitting there.

I had been away from the place where they had told me about my daughter for a while. It was good for my heart to have the break from the memories, but I longed to be there once more and in so many ways truly needed to be there again. I was going back to that place where I found shelter and to the ones I had grown to love and feel so safe with, who had been so instrumental in the valley.

I was thankful for Misty and her family who had taken me to the beach. God had placed them in my life during the time in between my days at the office. While I missed another holiday without a family of my own, I was able to allow the depth of the ocean to carry away even more of my pain. The tide replaced the sorrow with a new sense of hope once more. In the beauty of that morning and in the peacefulness of a time of individual worship of my Lord, joy was coming in waves.

I received a text message from Dr. Albert as I sat there, enjoying such a glorious morning, which said, *"I am thankful you are coming back."* I was thankful to be going back. In so many ways joy was returning to my life. I was struck by the similarities of the ocean's waves and the return of joy. It was not all complete in one simple wave. There were even differences in how they washed ashore. Some rolled in gently, softly finding their way to coming to rest higher upon the beach and some came in more quickly, pushed forward by the forces propelling them toward the soft, glistening sands of the beach. As beautifully as the waves were finding their way to the shore, joy was finding its way to my heart once more.

I truly celebrated Thanksgiving for the first time in my heart the following year. I was invited once more into the home and into the family of Lee and Gayle Williams. Along with their children and grandchildren we ate, played games, laughed and smiled. I didn't just enjoy the blessing of the day, I celebrated. The tide that had begun the previous Thanksgiving morning had brought with it healing waves of beauty that were fulfilled in this day.

My heart was created for relationship with God and with those people who He places in my life and it is beautiful. Love, is healing my heart so beautifully. It is the same divine crimson thread which has defined the entire valley. The horizon brings all these new joys to my heart every single morning, and still the horizon continues on, in the distance of each tomorrow God gives.

My purpose is no longer to simply be Elisabeth's mother, and raise her *"in the training and instruction of the Lord"* (EPH. 6:4). My purpose is no longer to be Jonathan's wife, and try to fulfill the function of that calling. It changed in the moment that the valley began. It took a while to find that purpose once more, but it came. Yes, it came, in walking with God. It came, in loving the people around me, and it came, doing the things I am doing every day.

I can't envision what tomorrow holds, but I know who holds my tomorrow. In knowing that, there will always be beauty. I have experienced God's grace to my heart. I have experienced His goodness in a terrible darkness and I have seen His love explode the boundaries of that valley so He shines so clearly in every day.

There are wonderful holidays, celebrated in both a heart of worship, and the joy of love. There are new smiles seen, new memories made, and new moments to share. Laughter and joy exist again. There will be love again one day too, somehow, in God's will and in his plan. There will be moments of experiencing all life holds with its ups and its downs, the good and the bad. The valley holds me captive no longer. For here in the moment and in each tomorrow there is truly life once more.

May our every breath
cry out for more of you Lord.
May we press in to you
and may our thirst for you
be ever growing.

Chapter 16

God's Love Remains

The beautiful crimson threads of God's love have woven a glorious tapestry of grace, across the darkness of a deep valley. His love created the foundations needed in my heart and in my life to take me through a journey that was tremendously difficult.

God's love has picked up the pieces of a shattered heart and created strengths and weaknesses where they have needed to be to continue to shape me into the person God wants me to become in Him. His love has brought peace. Through the wonderful days and the difficult ones, God has proven beyond any experience we encounter or challenge we face that always and still, God's love remains.

Within every situation, there are always two ways to look at things. My heart has a choice, to dwell and focus only on the negative and that which had been lost, or trust the God who has always known the end from the very beginning. My choices defined what God was able to do in my heart through the valley.

In the love of God which remains throughout all the moments of life, I have learned that indeed, *"all things work for good to those who love God and are called according to His purpose"* (Rom 8:28).

I didn't see it at the moment the nightfall of the valley was at it darkest point, but it came. The decisions I made had to be redeemed as only God could restore them. The decision to lead a child out of danger was one that any loving mother would make. The heartache when it was not enough to save her would be heartache any mother would feel. Even through the moments that still tinge my heart, the choice to go on and live once more is one that can be made in full and complete trust in the God whose love still remains.

So many times throughout the journey God has revealed that

while I may never know what the next moment holds, He will be with me in that moment. God hears and He answers prayer. Even though at times the answer may not be that which I had hoped for, as my will yields in love to His sovereignty, God will take that answer and redeem it into something that draws me even closer to Himself.

The precious healing of my wounded soul God will carry on throughout the rest of my days. I am grateful that it will for it is keeping me near His side. There is a beauty in the transformation that occurs because of the difficulties which propels us to find God. I am not the person I was before the valley began; all valleys change a heart.

God's word speaks to my heart that endings are always beginnings. One season of our life ends and another season begins. There were lessons to be learned in the journey of the valley. There were moments to come to bow in surrender before the throne of God and yield myself afresh to Him. There were moments which shine as gleaming hope that the darkness of the valley cannot and will never hide the God which a heart longs to find.

The borders of the valley fade into the distance of yesterdays. The beauty of the moment of today and the horizons of the joys of tomorrow shine gloriously in my heart. Through the love of God, there is the assurance that hope will forever continue. The heart which was once afraid to hope in anything because the wound was so deep can no longer fail to hope in the God who has proven without question His mercy and faithfulness.

Certainly, the journey was difficult and the darkness of the shadows of life's experiences left the human heart shaken for a season. Yet, the pathway leads once more to the steady and solid ground of faith renewed through God's mercy and His grace.

In the journey, the Lord guided each step through the darkness of the path I had to walk. When my heart was weary He allowed me to rest in Him. The green pastures and quiet waters within the valley were found in God alone.

When I was fearful, when I still am, God faithfully teaches that I can trust Him and those who He has placed in my life as holy reflections of His love. Stepping further in faith, I choose to allow my heart to remain open for all that God is doing within me, all that God is teaching me about Him. God has a glorious plan that is still yet to be in my life and I can trust Him to complete the purposes He has for me as I trusted Him to lead me out of my valley.

He taught me through looking glass moments that my heart needed Him. The things that brought me to my knees seeing the depth of my sin before His holiness drove me to the cross where my soul could be mended by the hand of a loving and merciful God. In this, God brought such solace to a heart which was hurting so deeply.

In the presence of the enemy of my soul who sought to destroy my heart, the God who I served beckoned me gently to come and sit by His side. Here at the table of God's grace I learned of His gentleness, here He gave peace and taught me of His faithfulness no matter the experiences of my life. Here at this table God gave the blessing of the oil of joy once more.

The beauty of the gift of today and the horizons of the joys of the tomorrows which lay ahead echo that still, God's love remains. His mercies fill my cup to the overflowing blessing of His boundless grace. Whatever my days hold He is more than enough.

The valley surely and beautifully comes to an end but the story of God's love remains. His goodness can never be limited by a season of pain, a moment of doubt or a journey through the difficult. God's goodness and His mercy have pursued me throughout the darkness the valley has held and if God has proven that, it will surely do the same as my life continues on into whatever He holds in store for my tomorrows.

My valley, while it is unimaginable and terrible, has successfully revealed God to my heart in such beautiful new facets of His love and His grace. It has taught me new principles of faith, it has opened the

Bible to me in wonderful new ways and it has caused my heart to long more deeply to serve Him with every fiber of my being.

There has been nothing good about what caused the valley. My tears have stained every ounce of the darkness it has held for my soul. The brokenness of my heart has been poured out upon the ground of this valley. My shattered heart was crushed under the pain and the deep ache of betrayal and destroyed promises and time and time again God revealed in even this, still His love remains.

Yes, those things which were meant to destroy me are, in the faithful mercy and grace of God, turning out to be the things which God is allowing to become my most profound blessings of faith. The weaknesses I now have because of it are instead becoming strengths as they keep me near to His side. The strengths that have formed because of the journey glorify God's remarkable love and grace in my life. As if shouting from the rooftops, my soul declares the praise and glory of my God and His faithfulness endures forever!

The crimson thread of God's love can be seen woven throughout the boundary of the depths of the darkness of the valley. When I could not see the gifts of God's faithfulness to His word in some respects, God taught me of His grace, His mercy. When I did not understand the questions which plagued my heart, the Lord taught me of the love of God which accepts my humanity. This valley, my valley, has proven to me as God promises to us all, the words of David in the 23rd Psalm.

PSALM 23

"The LORD is my shepherd, I lack nothing
He makes me lie down in green pastures,
he leads me beside quiet waters,
he refreshes my soul.
He guides me along the right paths
for his name's sake.
Even though I walk
through the darkest valley,

I will fear no evil,
for you are with me;
your rod and your staff,
they comfort me.
You prepare a table before me
in the presence of my enemies.
You anoint my head with oil;
my cup overflows.
Surely your goodness and love will follow me
all the days of my life,
and I will dwell in the house of the LORD
forever."

This story of my life has never really been my own. It is simply the story of the grace of God in the life of a soul. He wrote the pages of my life in some measure long before I ever existed – as He wrote the story of the death of His own Son on a cross so long ago to save me from my sin.

He did not simply save mankind. God saved me! This is the fullness of my story, just as it is the fullness of every story of a heart which accepts God's truth. As each one believes in Jesus and accepts Him as the Lord of life, repents for the heart of sin we all have, and turns away from that sin to serve Him, God writes his or her story of faith. He weaves His crimson threads of love through every moment that is faced and promises always to stay with us along the way.

I made a choice when I was ten to give my heart to a God who died for me. I made a choice four years ago to once more yield that heart and my life to God again. He is faithful, loving and good, even when I did not understand. His promises are sure and everlasting and what He has done for me He longs to do for us all.

"In him we were also chosen, having been predestined according to the plan of him who works out everything in conformity with the purpose of his will, in order that we, who were the first to put our hope in Christ,

131

might be for the praise of his glory."

How my heart rejoices that the final Chapter of what has been in this intense valley experience is simply the prologue to the greater story of my life. There are beautiful horizons yet to be known. There are wonderful journeys yet to be taken in this life.

Those pages yet to be written hold an even more precious story of what He will continue to compose each moment of my days. One glorious day my story will be lovingly handed back to Him as I breathe my last breath and enter eternity with Him. Until then, there is much left for my God to write in this beautiful story of life.

As a young girl I sat beside my dad on the back row of the sanctuary of our little church, reading the devotions they gave us after class had ended. It was here I read for the first time a passage of scripture which has always stood out to me in its beautiful description of the love and devotion of our Savior.

That passage is by far my favorite words my Savior has spoken to my heart. Ever since that day the words always make my heart say, *"Yes Lord, Yes!"* It also now contains the words which have lovingly declared the end of the valley and promises the beauty which waits ahead.

SONG OF SOLOMON 2:10-13

"My beloved spoke and said to me,

"Arise, my darling,

my beautiful one, come with me.

See! The winter is past;

the rains are over and gone.

Flowers appear on the earth;

the season of singing has come,

the cooing of doves

is heard in our land.

The fig tree forms its early fruit;

the blossoming vines spread their fragrance.

Arise, come, my darling;

my beautiful one, come with me."

The dawn of hope in Christ breaks softly over the horizon, its hues of golden rays casting a warm glow for the new joys waiting to be experienced and peace settles in my heart once more.

The chill of the night drifts silently away as I listen to the coo of the mourning dove sitting just outside the veranda wrapped in the warmth of the love of my Savior. A beautiful tapestry of woven threads that form a wonderful scene, each yarn has been significant to the final outcome of the portrait. The crimson threads of His love have brought me to this place, to this moment.

I suppose if I was to have decided my journey, I would have written a story filled with wonderful things, delightful memories and everlasting joy. In doing so, however, I would have missed the overwhelming blessing that my life has held and all the lessons along the way.

The peace of finding joy again is a remarkable witness of grace. No event, no circumstance, no encounter, no struggle and no pain can diminish the love of our God. Events do not define God; instead, it is God who will define events.

The love of God will never be limited, measured or in any way lessened by a valley or my response to the valley. God will always be there. Forever He will be faithful to His promise,

"the Lord your God goes with you; he will never leave you nor forsake you". (DEUTERONOMY 31:6)

God's promises of hope exceed all things a difficult journey may ever contain. God's goodness shines in the mercy and grace which far outweigh all that which may ever be known as a valley. The crimson threads of His love weave throughout any darkness or difficulty our life may hold and consistently show even in all that may ever occur, always and still, God's love remains.

Here in this moment, the past and the present meet. The future glistens gloriously within the realm of possibilities and I can trust that God has a purpose and He knows the plan. As I yield always and increasingly the throne of my heart to the Lord of all, then I will be guided along the path over hills, up mountains through more valleys onto steady paths and rest under the shadow of His wings as He causes me to come even closer to the glorious horizons of joy contained within my tomorrows in Christ.

"And now these three remain: faith, hope and love.
But the greatest of these is love." (1 COR 13:13)

Letter From The Author

Dear Friends,

Thank you for allowing me to share my heart with you through the pages of this book. No matter what life holds you can rest assured that God will always be there to walk the journey with you. He will never leave your side. In fact, He longs so much for you to reach out to Him.

While I suppose most of the readers of this story likely already have a relationship with Jesus Christ, there may be those who read this who have yet to make a commitment to the Lord who loved you so much He chose to die Himself so that you may live with Him for all eternity.

If you've never trusted Jesus as your personal Lord and Savior won't you please do that in our final moments together? You see, we have all sinned. Jesus, God's own Son, died in our place so that we may have eternal life. It's as simple as a prayer, turning from your sin and surrendering your life to Him, every moment of every day. Would you please pray with me?

Father God, I have sinned. I fail. I recognize that you are Holy and Jesus is the one and only way to salvation. I ask you to come into my heart and make me new. Please be my Lord and my Savior. Please redeem the ashes of my life into all that you choose. I surrender my heart, everything I have and everything I am to you now. I will live for you the rest of my days. In the precious name Jesus, I ask. Amen.

If you've prayed that, you are a new creation in Christ and heaven is rejoicing with you. Would you please write to me and let me know? If my story has somehow helped in your own journey, I'd love to know that as well.

Thank you again for spending some time with me. May God's blessings and favor always be yours.

Sincerely,
Amy

About the Author

Amy E. (Elisabeth) Tobin is a pen name. The info about the author is about the person behind the name.

Sound Confusing? No worries. Please continue reading.

The pen name is used by Amy to provide as much protection as possible to the people who were touched in some measure by the events that began a journey.

This name was chosen because *"Amy"* means *"loved."* Elisabeth is a family name and Tobin means *"the Lord is good"* in Hebrew. So each time a person says Amy Tobin, that individual is speaking a blessing into the life of the author.

Amy shares her story to glorify the God who chose to spare her life as well as to encourage, inspire and help others find hope in God for their own circumstances of life. When she isn't writing or speaking Amy enjoys a simple, quiet life.

So, a bio about Amy is, in essence, really a bio about the mercy, love and redemption of her Savior, Jesus Christ.